HEARTS IN ZION

Other books by Bruce Hopkins:

Spirits in the Field: An Appalachian Family History

Bright Wings to Fly: An Appalachian Family in the Civil War

Hearts in Zion

Steel, Coal, and an Appalachian Family

Bruce Hopkins

WIND PUBLICATIONS
2009

International Standard Book Number 978-1-893239-88-3
Library of Congress Control Number 2008943534

First edition

Front cover: Greasy Creek Coal Camp, 1928

By the rivers of Babylon,
> There we sat down and there we wept
> When we remembered Zion.
On the willows there
> We hung up our harps.
For there our captors
> Asked us for songs,
And our tormentors asked for mirth, saying,
> "Sing us one of the songs of Zion!"

How could we sing the Lord's song
> In a foreign land?
If I forget you, O Jerusalem,
> Let my right hand wither!
Let my tongue cling to the roof of my mouth
> If I do not remember you...

— From *Psalm* 137

Rissie

Contents

Illustrations & Photographs

January 1913

*T*hrough the frost-covered window, Malissa could see the little girl pacing on the big front porch of Harrison's house, in spite of the chill that surrounded her, the chill that found its way between floorboards of the house and under the doors. As the night closed in, even the walls seemed to seep the cold. With so many people coming and going, there was no point in plugging the drafts, and although the fireplaces were roaring and the kitchen stove glowing red-hot, it was not warm in the home. Malissa wondered if that was because the weather was so bad or because the Hopkinses had just buried Mammy and lost the heart of their clan.

For that matter, not only were they the poorer for Mammy's loss, all of Greasy Creek had lost one of its legends, and the Hopkins kitchen was overwhelmed with food as matrons from up and down the creek continued to bring dishes to nourish the mourners.

A funeral in winter is a hard thing for anyone, Malissa thought, but it must be harder on these people, especially for Rissie, who continued her pacing despite the bitter wind. She was Mammy's granddaughter and her darling, and for Rissie, whose infirmities Mammy dismissed as inconsequential, the old woman was her life.

Malissa wondered what the clan would be like after Mammy, and wondered how Greasy Creek itself would change.

1

It had changed enough already, with coal mines opening all over Pike County and work available everywhere. There were rumors a big steel company would soon build a town here, on Greasy Creek. A town on Greasy Creek? What would Mammy have thought of something so strange, so unbelievable?

Mammy was a truer link to the past than even the old Civil War soldiers who still lived, and not only was she Harrison's mother and the unchallenged matriarch of the Hopkins clan, she was much the surrogate grandmother to everyone on the creek. In spite of her age, she was as popular with the young people as she was respected by the elders. Half the weddings on Greasy Creek took place or were celebrated at her home. Rissie, Harrison's club-footed daughter, whose cleft palate was now repaired as much as could be done, found purpose and sanctuary at Mammy's house. Malissa knew Mammy's funeral would give Rissie respite only briefly from the yahoos who would soon again mimic her unsteady gait and whistling speech in the cruel pantomimes of children.

"Lila," Malissa said to Harrison's wife. "That child's going to catch her death out there. You want me to bring her in?"

"She won't come in Aunt Malissy," Lila replied, shaking her head at the sight of her daughter crossing in front of the window. "I don't know what's to become of her. She's tired; she ain't slept a wink since Mammy died."

"What if I take her home with me tonight? She won't get no rest here with everbody comin' and goin'."

Lila looked at the crowd in her home and conceded that the sleeping arrangements would be difficult. Less than half the guests had departed after the funeral.

"She needs her sleep," Lila said. "But I ain't sure she'll go."

"You let me try," Malissa said as she pulled on her coat.

That could be the best thing for Rissie, Lila thought. If anyone can comfort her, it would be Aunt Malissa. It pleased Lila that Mammy and Malissa had gotten along well, since Mammy had little regard for Ezekiel Prater, Malissa's father-in-law.

For years, Mammy blamed him, or at least his Union regiment, for capturing her beloved Confederate Uncle Joe Hopkins during the War and leading him to his doom in the flatlands of Kentucky, far from the mountains. But Mammy had softened toward the Praters after Ezekiel died, and to some extent, even before. She had to admit that Zeke was a good man, and she was grateful he allowed the Hopkinses to continue burying their dead on his land after he bought the property. But she was, and everyone knew it, an unreconstructed Confederate until her death.

That might have explained why Mammy and Malissa were close; Malissa's father was also a Confederate and a comrade of Joe in the same regiment. And even Mammy would have confessed that her Uncle Lum, a brother to Joe, had been a Union soldier in the same regiment as Zeke, but thankfully not present at Joe's capture. But some things die hard, and before Zeke died in 1906, Mammy would rarely come inside Malissa's house when she decorated the cemeteries.

Both women took a special pride in the two cemeteries on Melissa's land: the older one, where the first Hopkinses on Greasy Creek were buried, and the newer one, where both the Hopkinses and Praters now slept. They were fiercely protective of the graves and both imparted that responsibility to Rissie; it was a charge she understood in spite of her age.

Rissie was not quite nine years old.

As Malissa went out to fetch the little girl, Lila could not repress a smile. Malissa and Mammy were so much alike: both could cuss like soldiers, both loved to laugh, and both smoked corncob pipes that Lila knew they surreptitiously offered Rissie when she was out of Lila's sight. Most importantly, she knew they both loved her tiny, crippled daughter. Lila knew Malissa could never replace Mammy for Rissie, but Malissa's rambunctious household would help take Rissie's mind off her loss, at least for tonight.

Malissa eased the screen door shut. The little girl was still pacing and did not see her approach in the twilight. Malissa looked quizzically at Rissie's fingers tapping on the long stem of a pipe as she walked.

"You going to smoke that or play a tune on it, baby?" Malissa asked softly. "Ain't it a little cold to be out here?"

Surprised, Rissie looked up at Malissa and then down at the object in her hand.

"It's Mammy's," she said softly. "It ain't that cold."

"Your mam just made some doughnuts." Malissa remembered doughnuts to be one of Rissie's favorites because they were sweet and tender to her reconstructed palate.

"I ain't hungry," Rissie barely whispered.

"Well, if you ain't hungry, you want to light up Mammy's pipe?" Malissa winked conspiratorially.

Rissie's face brightened, but she looked apprehensively toward the door.

"Well, hell, I don't reckon we can smoke here," Malissa said, looking to her left and right. "Tell you what, sweetheart; you go home with me tonight and we'll sit by the fire and smoke and talk."

"Did Mommy say I could go?"

"She sure did," Malissa answered cheerfully. "Lord Jesus, you'd have to sleep at the foot of the bed if you stayed here. I don't know about you, but I never did like somebody's old toenails scratching my back. But let's go get us a doughnut first, what do you say?"

In a few minutes, after her mother had bundled her against the wind, Rissie walked into the evening gloom down the twisting Gardner Fork road. Malissa watched Rissie closely to see if she needed to hold her hand to steady her, but she knew Rissie would be too proud to ask for help in spite of her clubfoot.

As they approached the forks of Greasy Creek, Rissie became subdued; Malissa's house stood on the same land the

Hopkins compound occupied decades before, overlooking the field where Uncle Joe's infamous brother Elisha, once the head of the clan, raised horses before the War came, before the world he ruled was lost.

Elisha, "Old Lige," as everyone knew him, was Rissie's great-grandfather, and had died almost nine years before, not long after Rissie was born. He had four wives, three at the same time, and countless children, and he loved them all. He was the central character in most of Mammy's stories, but Rissie wondered who would want to hear them now that she was gone.

"What's troublin' you, child?" Malissa asked her.

"I don't...I...I'm just...worried."

"'Bout what?" Malissa gently demanded, puzzled by her answer. "You ain't got nothing to worry about."

"About the stories."

"What stories?"

"The stories Mammy told me."

Malissa could see Rissie's gloved fingers still tapping on the pipe stem. That's what she's doing, Malissa thought; she's counting out the stories.

"She told me never to forget them," Rissie said. "She told me to tell them to the family, so they won't forget."

Rissie took a deep breath; the cold air rushed into her lungs and she coughed. "I ain't sure I remember all of 'em. Mammy told me so many. I'm afraid I'll forget."

"Not you, baby girl," Malissa reassured her. "Old Mammy knew you'd never forget."

"But what if I do, Aunt Malissy?"

In the fading light, Malissa could see Rissie's lower lip tremble. Her upper lip, fixed by the scar from her surgery, barely moved. "What if I can't remember? Nobody wants to listen to me anyway. Everybody's bragging about their old jobs."

"You don't need to worry, little girl," Malissa replied. "You ain't going to forget. Mammy saw a light in you, sweetheart, and it won't go out. She told me that many times, and as long as I live, you can always come to me when you think you're forgettin' what she told you. I know a lot of those stories, too; I seen a lot of it happen."

Rissie looked again at the pipe and carefully placed it in the pocket of her coat. Apparently satisfied, she picked up the pace and marched steadily beside Malissa as they crossed Elisha's field. In the gathering darkness, they passed the big, new house of Harmon Robinson. She could see people in the house standing by the fireplace and most of the windows were illuminated. Kinfolk were staying there too; Harmon was one of Elisha's many sons.

"I just want Mammy to be proud of me," Rissie said.

"That she is, baby girl; that she is. She may be gone and can't speak to you anymore, but she'll always be proud."

"You reckon they really are ghosts?" Rissie asked. "I mean, Mammy said they were. I asked her what ghosts were and she said just spirits. She said sometimes people just stay around for a while after they die to look out for their family."

"Why sure there are," Malissa immediately replied. "They just can't speak to us anymore. They wouldn't try to scare us or nothin', but they're around."

"How do you know?"

"Well, you just know it, baby. You just know."

"Do soldier boys come home if they die somewhere else, like Uncle Joe did?"

"Why yes they do; they come back to where they were happy."

"And those people on the Titanic? They were so far out on the water; did they make it home?"

This child is wise beyond her years, Malissa thought.

"I 'spect they did. Ghosts ain't tied down by the bodies, you know. They come back to where they were the happiest. Hell, up on Ripley Knob, Old Lige is probably makin' a batch of whiskey right now. Him and his Indians could be havin' a big whoop-te-do for all we know. We can't see it of course; we ain't really supposed to."

"He died just after I was born. I wish I'd knowed him, but it seems like I do."

"That's 'cause Mammy taught you right."

"Aunt Malissy," Rissie spoke solemnly. "If I ever tell the stories wrong, will you let me know?"

"Yes, I will, darlin'. I surely will."

"I just want Mammy to be proud of me, even if she can't talk to me no more."

They exited the field and crossed the wider main Greasy Creek road to the bridge that led to Malissa's house. The winter sky had completely darkened, but Rissie could see ice glistening under the bridge. She could also see snowflakes beginning to fall as they walked up Malissa's wide front steps and went inside. Passersby, if there were any on that frigid evening, would have seen only their shadows through the frosty panes, as if the young girl and the woman were themselves the ghosts they spoke of.

Indeed, on Ripley Knob, the ghost of Elisha Hopkins could have been making the whiskey that made him famous. Or he could have been working on the cabin he and his brother had built a lifetime before, the cabin the brothers built to impress their father, the cabin where they started their families, the same cabin where Elisha took his last breath on this earth after a life of legend.

Or there could have been spectral lovers at the cabin; there had been many when its hearth was warm and children played outside its threshold. One of them would never live to braid her daughter's hair or see her grandchildren, although some of the old people on Greasy Creek would swear that they had seen her walk off the mountains on early winter evenings as she went in search of her husband and child.

But if they existed, all of them, all the souls now in peril of becoming unremembered, all the remnants of lost dreams and forgotten days, all of them looked toward Malissa's house and the glow of her fire and the young girl not yet nine years old, the child whom they would have known to be their best hope, their only hope, the only heart on Greasy Creek or anywhere on that cold January planet they could depend on to tell their stories faithfully and keep their memories alive long after the morning came and the darkness fell away and the sunlight returned to burn into nothingness the last, fragile ephemera of the unseen and unknowable shades.

Cities of the Hills

I would not look at them, those pale specters that beckoned to me in the corner of my eye as I drove through what was left of the town on the way to somewhere, anywhere else. I looked straight ahead and pretended they did not exist, and I felt no remorse for my disregard. Now I try to find them, to remember, to capture an image here and there from the pixels they may have imprinted on my brain, but without success.

They will sometimes visit me in dreams, but I am far removed from the child I was when I first heard their stories and I cannot will them to show themselves on the obliterated streets they once walked. They will not pardon my dismissal of them so long ago, after I grew up and forgot that I once sat enraptured as my grandmother told me of the town, of the mine, of the people who lived there and of those who lived there a hundred years before the mine came.

I am not entirely alone in this; refugees from ten thousand other coal towns will tell you the same thing. We left the forgotten places of our births in the Appalachian Mountains to find work, to make a living where we could, since home could not support us anymore. As the years passed, although we could not forget the earth where we first breathed, we know the earth has come to forget us, like rejected lovers who see through hurt-filled eyes and cannot forgive their abandonment.

But I know they are there, and I sought them in an unlikely place, but unlikely only because it was not in the mountains, as I drove through the steel gates of Cleveland, Ohio's Lake View Cemetery in the spring of 2008. I had been there before, some forty years before, but the circumstances were different. In 1967, I lived in one of the hillbilly enclaves of Akron, the Tire Capital of the World just south of Cleveland, when I received notice from my Kentucky draft board that I was to report for a physical examination. The Selective Service System allowed me, along with hundreds of other hillbilly boys, to take our orders to the induction station closest to our work, so I got up before daylight and drove up to my appointment.

I knew the way. I worked second shift at Ford Motor Company's huge Cleveland Stamping Plant, doing the same job my father once did there: feeding flat sheets of new steel into a giant machine that smashed them into approximate contours of doors and fenders. I would pull the sheets off a never-ending pile and place them into the jaws of a giant press that demanded more and more food for its oily, never-satisfied maw.

At first, it was a physical challenge for my scrawny frame just to keep the metal flowing; I had never worked so hard in my life, but as my muscles adapted, strength, or the lack of it, was no longer the problem. Instead, the challenge became mental. The sheer monotony of dong the same thing over and over for eight hours or more was overwhelming. I began to see why labor strikes were common: they provided a break from mind-numbing routine. Sometimes, the slightest infraction of union rules provoked a sudden walkout, and I suspect the line supervisors welcomed the occasional stoppage as much as the workers.

It was never a surprise when one line or another walked off. I would follow the rest of the men, even though I was never a rabid union partisan. Tension between labor and management was not unusual to me; I had grown up with it in the coal fields.

With me on the lines were other pilgrims from the mountains: Eastern Kentucky boys and West Virginia boys and a few from Virginia and Tennessee. They had come north, like me, following paths established even before the births of our fathers, whose previous journeys we largely emulated. We were not the first generation to leave the hills; fathers, grandfathers, and some great-grandfathers preceded us, looking for work or perhaps escape, when the sustaining culture of our ancestors, an ancient constitution of trust and loyalty, was shattered in blood and fire.

Few of us knew that many of our people became nomads when the Civil War brought a close to the cherished independence and self-sufficiency of our ancestors. I may have known it, but had forgotten my lessons. Like the others, I knew merely the unwritten rule that for at least part of our lives we would have to live away from home.

I lived among my clan in South Akron, where most of the city's hillbillies lived. It would not have been unfair to call it an enclave, even though its boundaries were undeclared. At the time, we were not trusting of the outside world; some vague but universal misgiving preordained our relationships with people who did not speak our dialect. We were most comfortable among our own kind and did not venture far from them.

Hillbillies then were like any other minority group and we were susceptible to ridicule. "Hillbilly" was a pejorative term; people who referred to us that way were not congratulating us on our ancestry. We winced when we heard it used, since it was only a notch above the standard opprobrium for African-Americans.

Country music, which provided the anthem for our race, had not reached the broad acceptance it has now and "hillbilly" had not yet been claimed by the new generation of singers who now happily style themselves such, even if they come from Los Angeles and have never drawn a bucket of water from a well carved by their great-grandfathers.

I wasn't a fan of country music and I cared little for sequin-suited, pompadour-coiffed Porter Wagoner types who were its gods. Besides, only a few radio stations in Northeast Ohio would play it. I had other preferences, but I was still a hillbilly. I was reticent about my language and would not speak too loudly for fear of revealing my origin. Much of my northern family lost the soft lilt of their native voices in the necessity of conforming to life in the fast pace of industrial Ohio or other states where work could be found. Those of us who eventually succumbed to life in the North, voting citizens of Michigan or Indiana or Ohio, had children who were not shaped and molded by the creeks and hollows where we grew up. That culture became as alien to them as the obscure place in Southeast Asia where we expected to be sent after our physicals.

I had a deferment in 1967. I was 2-S because I was a student. I still had to take the examination and I was not sure my deferment would last. When the war began in earnest after the Tonkin Resolution, married men soon lost their deferments. Manpower demands escalated with our country's involvement, and what was once a place we could not have found on a map now became a major threat to our futures.

The country had changed since I began high school in the fall of 1960. After President Kennedy was assassinated, Vietnam began appearing on the Huntley-Brinkley Report with increasing regularity. By 1967, every American boy my age knew where it was and, eventually, nearly all of us wished it had never existed.

After high school, I spent a year in college in Kentucky, but jobs were scarce and tuition was expensive. I had no choice but to move away and went to Akron, where my family had emigrated and where jobs were plentiful. I enrolled in the University of Akron, a municipal school that catered to workers' long hours, and I took jobs that allowed me to work around the classes I needed. The Rust Belt had not yet formed and I could easily find a job to accommodate my changing schedule at school, sometimes from semester to semester. When I received my SSS orders, I was attending lectures on English literature in the morning and flinging sheet metal at night.

The envelope containing my orders came in the same envelope as the dreaded "Greetings" that often followed suit, but I was not that worried when it arrived in the mail. Still, I had little confidence my 2-S status would last much longer. It was not reassuring that I was standing in line with hundreds of other boys my age, some of whom would soon be starting the last journey of their lives. My discomfiture was eased a bit by the freedom of a whole day off from school and work. My boss told me that I couldn't make it to work on time, I shouldn't come at all and I expected to be there all day.

I arrived at the Cleveland Federal Building at six in the morning, but by one o'clock, I was released. I was surprised, and found myself with the better part of a day away from books and factories. I decided to spend it at a cemetery and I had a reason.

In the city park of Pikeville, the county seat of Pike County, Kentucky, there is a historical marker noting that James A. Garfield was made a brigadier general there for his military success in the Big Sandy Valley during the Civil War. The Big Sandy River flows past Pikeville to the Ohio and for nearly a hundred years it was the main shipping route into Eastern Kentucky. One of Garfield's feats during his campaign was to commandeer a riverboat to bring supplies to his men from the Union base downriver. He had been a river pilot in Ohio and used his skills when the steamer captains refused to take their boats up the flooding Big Sandy.

I had been ambivalent about Garfield, since he was Union and, like any Southern boy, I was mesmerized by the Lost Cause. When my grandmother told me about my Civil War family, I paid little heed to the Union side, but in fact more of my ancestors were Union than Confederate. What I did not appreciate then was that my county, on the border of two warring countries, suffered as much as any theater of the War, although no major battles were fought there. The suffering was personal; almost every family was split and the divisions took generations to heal. As I learned more about Garfield and his deeds, I began to admire the Union conqueror of the Big Sandy Valley.

When I first read the marker, I was surprised that any claim to fame could be associated with my obscure county, but it was true that a future President of the United States was thrust into national recognition from my little county seat. In 1862, the Union was losing the War, at least in the press, and any good news was gratefully disseminated in the Northern papers. John Hay, one of Abraham Lincoln's most trusted advisers, saw an opportunity with Garfield and advised the President to make him a general and then ask him to resign from the Army and return to Ohio politics. That fell into place, and few Ohioans know or would deign to admit that one of their many Presidents began his career in tiny Pikeville, Kentucky.

Pikeville is a relatively prosperous city for the coal fields, but it is certainly not in the same league as Cleveland or Akron. It has been the county seat since 1823, when the first Hopkins in Pike County, my ancestor Cornelius, appeared on the county tax rolls. It is one of the largest towns in Eastern Kentucky, but it is not my hometown, although in 1967, I often intimated it was. My hometown was a largely obliterated coal town called Greasy Creek, named after the desultory stream that meanders through it to the Big Sandy. For fear of further classifying myself as a hillbilly, I rarely mentioned that fact. At least "Pikeville" sounded cosmopolitan; "Greasy Creek" certainly did not.

But few of the mountain boys who worked with me in the factories and mills of Ohio talked about the dead places of their births. Most of them, like me, came from old coal towns as lifeless and forgotten as Greasy Creek. A West Virginia boy, also a Ford worker, went through the examination process with me, and we talked, almost conspiratorially, about our former homes as we moved from station to station. He was from a town called Gassaway and I felt a kinship because of that fact alone; the name of his town sounded as ridiculous as mine.

After we were released, I asked him if he wanted to visit a cemetery with me. He was incredulous.

"A cemetery? Are you shittin' me? You wanna go to a God damn cemetery? We'll all friggin' be there soon enough."

My friend had no deferment; if he passed, he would soon be reporting for active duty. The doctors found no reason to reject him and told him as much.

"Well, what are you going to do the rest of the day?" I asked.

"I'm goin' to Billy Lee's and get drunk," he replied. "Why the hell not?"

I should have expected as much; Billy Lee's Lounge, on South Main Street, was the mother church of Akron's hillbilly bar life. Most of the West Virginia and Kentucky boys paid homage to the bottle there and I'm certain my friend arrived early enough to ensure a memorable toot. In a few weeks, he got his orders and I never saw him again. The next year, I went back to Kentucky. I have forgotten his last name and I do not know if it appears on the Wall.

Forty years later, nothing is the same in Ohio. Akron has lost the infamous smell of tires curing in the thousands of molds that produced them. At one time, the aroma of that process would greet travelers fifty miles from town, but no tires are made, "built" in rubber shop jargon, in Akron anymore. Cleveland is cleaner as well; it has lost the sulfurous atmosphere of the steel mills, since only one now exists under strict pollution control, and no longer do blackened chimneys belch smoke day and night from the Kentucky coal that fired its furnaces. But both places still yearn for their distinctive smells, because they meant jobs, which now are gone to other places where labor is cheaper and the environment is more easily assaulted.

Forty years before, the jobs and the pollution were a given, and perhaps the only connection between these times and now is the fact that its young people again face a war in an alien place where American boys should not be dying.

15

Hearts in Zion

In 1967, I went to Lake View Cemetery to visit the monu-
mental tomb of President Garfield and I found its porous, brown
sandstone black from the soot of the mills. I did not know then
that coal from Greasy Creek had fired one of those mills. Not far
from Garfield rested the great robber baron John D. Rockefeller,
whose grave I also visited because I was there. I strolled around
a bit afterward. The statuary and funereal markers of the vast
cemetery were interesting, but after an hour of wandering, I
went back to Akron. I had no other reason to be there and I had
assignments to complete before classes resumed in the morning.

In 2008, I came to Lake View Cemetery for a different purpose and I knew well that Kentucky coal was responsible for the
soot of forty years before. It was one of many things I had
learned, or relearned, in forty years. I had planned to come the
previous year, which was not a year of any special remembrance,
although it should have been. 2007 was the ninetieth anniversary of the United States entry into World War I and on
Veterans Day only one American soldier of that conflict still
lived. A few stories were published about him, but there was an
obvious lack of interest in the Great War. I suspect it simply had
to do with the numbers: "ninety years" does not have the same
cachet of "a century," but the press missed an opportunity by
not doing more with his story. It would be unlikely he would be
available for the more memorable location in ten years.

The cemetery was open when I arrived, but I was deeply disappointed that the office was closed. I needed help in finding
two graves among the thousands of sites and I did not expect to
be able to come back in another forty years. Although thinking I
would at least try, I resigned myself to the improbability of
finding them. After keeping my convertible top up on the drive
up from Akron, I dropped it to drive through the cemetery. It
was warm and pleasant enough and I could see the markers
more easily. I drove slowly, twisting my head at anything that
looked promising, but after an hour of fruitless searching, I
finally admitted defeat.

Maybe they don't want their stories told, I thought.

Since I was there, I decided to retrace my steps of forty years before to the still-stained memorial to the Twentieth President of the United States. It had not moved from its commanding spot and neither had Rockefeller's grave, marked by a pristine white obelisk that seemed freshly scrubbed, as it probably was. It looked as new in 2008 as it did in 1967. By contrast, Garfield's tomb still did not appear to have ever been cleaned. I wondered how far the soot from coal mined by my father and grandfather had penetrated into the soft stone of his memorial. It was still inspiring and was a contrast to the sterile plot where the bones of John D. Rockefeller lay. There was a desiccated wreath of fresh flowers in front of the Rockefeller obelisk, askew as if it had fallen over and someone had hastily reset it on its three flimsy metal legs. There were other people on the cemetery and no one had bothered to straighten it. Having no reason to extend any charity to the greatest robber baron of them all, I ignored it as well.

On a flat above Rockefeller's grave, a fierce warrior Gabriel watches over the grave of John Hay, whose advice to Lincoln had propelled Garfield on his journey to the presidency. It is shrouded by foliage and sits in quiet repose. Not far away is the grave of Franklin Rockefeller, who would not be buried in the same plot as his brother John D. Many famous graves in Lake View are clearly marked for the visitor, but I knew the graves I sought would have no reason to be. Since the sky was darkening and my quest was over, I stopped to put up my top and begin my return trip to Akron.

When I opened my door, I was stunned to find I had parked directly in front of the graves I sought. I was even more surprised to find they were practically side-by-side. Near the pavement, two massive black cenotaphs stood mutely, bearing simple inscriptions: "Corrigan" on one and "McKinney" on the other, holding for eternity the ordered nomenclature of one of Cleveland's nearly-forgotten steel companies. Behind both stones were the graves of family members, denoted by simple markers for each grave. Behind the Corrigan marker, however, one stone denoted the remains of two people, one buried on top of the other, exactly twenty years apart. Several of the Corrigan markers had the same tragic 1900 date and near them was the stone of James W. Corrigan, who was known in Cleveland as "Captain Jim."

All the more ironic, I thought, considering how his family died.

In the same position behind the McKinney cenotaph was the grave of Captain Jim's best friend, Price McKinney. Beside Captain Jim was his best friend's worst enemy: "Young Jim" Corrigan, Jimmy, Captain Jim's only son. I had learned much about the Corrigans and the McKinneys since I last visited Lake View, but I was surprised to find the graves in such proximity. But they were why I had come to Lake View Cemetery again.

The grass covering the plots was trimmed professionally and precisely and nothing was out of place, nothing to indicate the spot was regularly visited by anyone. The graves lay in elegant detachment, perhaps as forgotten and little more important to modern-day Cleveland than a lost grave on a hillside on Greasy Creek, which only one of the people buried there had ever seen.

I stood for a while longer and breathed in the air, so much cleaner now than I remembered it.

So these are their graves, I thought. Maybe they want their stories told after all.

*   *   *

Aside from World War I, there was another anniversary in 2007, and war tinged that celebration as well. Forty years before, my generation was part of the Summer of Love. We had not heard of it in the Kentucky hills and the term had not yet been coined, but all of us were aware of something happening to the national psyche as we turned our heads and coughed for Army doctors.

I passed my physical in 1967, but my deferment held and I decided to return home to re-enroll in tiny Pikeville College and complete my English degree. I had spent three years in the North and that was enough. Kentucky coal was beginning to sell again and although I would not receive the industrial wages I had enjoyed in Ohio, I knew I could find a job to pay for my last year of school. Additionally, because my father had some political clout, I had a teaching job awaiting me when I graduated.

I still did not want to live on Greasy Creek.

Like thousands of boys who left the mountains in the Sixties, I was the product of an economy that began dying with its birth. All of us knew the desperate cycles of the coal industry, the ups and downs that attracted and repelled workers in a timeless ebb and flow. In the early part of the Twentieth Century, literally thousands of coal towns sprang up in Kentucky and other states where coal was king. At that time, our ancestors did not know the impermanence of the towns that were built for them. Except for a very few, coal towns were merely part of company logistics, little more than warehouse space for foreign workers since there were too few native workers available.

Until 1914, when war in Europe cut off immigration, shiploads of human cargo disembarked at East Coast ports and headed for the mines and mill towns of America, where jobs awaited them. The war put labor at a premium, since there was always more work than men, but the stemming of the tide was merciful in one respect: had any more workers arrived before the economy collapsed in 1929, there would have been a greater number of desperate men and starving families to suffer the Depression.

Throughout the Thirties and afterward, except for the need for labor during World War II as men were called away, there were now too many men for the available jobs in the coal fields.

Even in the good times, when the demand for coal saw resurgence during the Eisenhower years, there was little surplus in the job market, as mechanization replaced strong arms and backs.

Although the economy had improved in Pike County by the Sixties, the labor supply was equivalent to demand and few coal companies were hiring. It was a far cry from the days when coal companies would shamelessly send agents to other coal fields to lure miners away. My father had a good job in Pike County's Republic Steel mine, but he did not want me to become a miner, even though there were few alternatives in Eastern Kentucky. So like him, I went north to find work and in fact worked in the same plant as he once did, but when he was called back to his mining job, he returned to the place he loved most. For me, it was a calculated risk to go home. I was leaving a land of opportunity for a tired place that I did not want to live in or even admit I was from. I wasn't entirely sure why I came back.

Now, Pikeville is booming and Pike County is helping feed the country's gluttonous demand for coal, although fewer men are working now than when my father went underground. Instead, the most popular method of extracting coal is to blow up the tops of mountains that sat in peace for millennia and push the debris into the hollows below. Real miners, men who would challenge the mountains from deep inside them, are disappearing; demolition experts and bulldozer operators now do most of the work at less risk and more profit for the coal companies. The land pays the awesome price for this work; the Appalachians are the oldest mountains in the world and had not changed in millions of years, yet now the moon comes up on an altered landscape every month.

"Why are they doing this?" an old high school friend of mine who had retired in the North asked as he saw a mountaintop removal mine for the first time. "Can't they get the coal any other way?"

He remembered his father, who worked with my father, in the honorable profession of underground mining. Both our fathers were gone, but we remembered well the pride they had in their work and stories of the brotherhood of men who toiled in darkness. He shook his head at the loss of mountains once thought immovable and eternal.

Some of the boys who stayed on in Ohio returned as the factories began to close, but finding no work, went on south. My friend was fortunate enough to have worked long enough to retire with a pension, and decided to come home to live out his life, but he went south himself, not to find work, but perhaps to find peace. Greasy Creek had changed many times since he left; it wasn't the same anymore, but it had also changed many times since the first white men came there two centuries ago.

In 1967, I had not thought much about Greasy Creek's history, in spite of my grandmother's stories. She told me of the mines and of what had happened long before the mines came, but I had other thoughts. I had learned enough of what had happened to the hills that I wanted no part of it. When the white men arrived, the mountains were as safe and sheltering as they had been for eons. Then the timber speculators came in the 1880's and the hillsides were denuded. After the Civil War money was hard to come by, and after the timber was taken, coal speculators came in with money to seduce those who had held out. By 1900, the die was cast; the railroad began arriving to haul away our birthrights, which our ancestors had sold on the cheap. They did not know the fate to which they had damned their progeny.

Coal was all my generation knew; it was all my father and grandfather knew. It was the same throughout the coal fields and not just in the Appalachians; the far West has its worked out seams and vanished coal towns as well, and all over America such towns came and went. No one really knows, but some estimates claim *twenty thousand* of them were built in the roughly forty-year period before and after 1900. Over ten thousand alone were built in the Southern Appalachian coal fields, and that can be proven, but outside my mountains, the towns were not shoehorned into tiny valleys that might once have been the domain of a single family or clan. More importantly, they did not cause the sea change in culture that "camps," as they were known, forced on the people who lived in those wild hills.

The collection of houses and buildings that supported the great mine on Greasy Creek was known as a camp and during the Sixties, that's how I viewed it. Today, I want to think of it as a town.

Camps were demonstrably transient places, with cheaply built housing, dirt streets, and little institutional effort to improve the lives of the residents. Towns were usually places established before the coal industry arrived, like Pikeville, which had been a busy port on the Big Sandy for nearly a century. Only the largest towns still survive, but only because they were large, and now, without company sponsorship, are only a shell of what they were during their boom years.

Greasy Creek was not a large camp by any means, but the president of the McKinney Steel Company wanted to make it a model community. It had a flower club, fraternal lodges, a brass band and a baseball team. It was a town, but little of it remains; barely enough to show for all the loss, all the heartbreak, and all the stories that will never be told of that deserted place.

I watched it disappear when I lived there, barely noting its steady dissolution, since so much of it was already gone. The few old houses that lined the narrow alleys came down as time passed, although there was no method to the process. It was more feral, like when a wild animal dies and pieces of its carcass are torn away by scavengers bit by bit, until little more than dry bones remain. The comparison may be apt. I've been told Greasy Creek was wild in its youth.

I didn't see it die; that happened long before I was born. My generation came along after the era of the great coal towns collapsed. We saw what came afterward, what always comes after death: the slow decomposition of the living thing it was into a loose amalgam of rotted parts and then into the nothingness of the space it once occupied. But the death of my town was crueler because it died young and, aside from its ruins, would have no stone, no marker to indicate where it once flourished or that it existed at all. Its untimely death was the final blow to my people, who never recovered from the loss.

When the town of Greasy Creek was built, it was much like others of the era. It had no real name because none were given them. For post offices, names had to be procured, but they were often named ceremonially for a financier who made the investment in the town. Edgewater and Hellier, two other vanished coal camps near Greasy Creek, were named for rich East Coast moneymen who never sat foot there. I often wondered why Greasy Creek was not named "McKinney," for the man who had built it, but when the post office was established in 1920, he named it for the creek instead.

Internally to the corporations that built them, camps were merely numbers: Camp Number One or Camp Number Two. Some were designated by location on the creeks where they were built: Upper Camp or Lower Camp, but they were usually nothing more than inventory numbers on an account's ledger, locations for the allocated expense of storing the labor force and built, maintained or discarded according to the needs of the company.

The orderliness of these places, so different from the rugged hills where they were inserted, made coal camps resemble military installations more than anything. Everything was geared toward the efficient movement of men and materiel to complete the mission, which was to make war on the mountains and the rich coal seams they grudgingly yielded. And like any military operation, the cost of achieving the mission was often onerous.

In 1968, I came back changed to Pike County, with strange music ringing in my ears, and I found the county had changed too. There was a minor burst of prosperity in the coal fields and the redundant, utilitarian, square camp houses that dotted the hills became unfashionable. Greasy Creek was no exception, and many of the remaining structures were replaced by one-story, cheaply built, Jim Walter homes. Real bathrooms began to appear, replacing outdoor toilets; wiring was hidden inside walls and fuse boxes placed inside the houses instead of on porches, where the elements had rusted the cabinets into the color of dried blood.

Natural gas heaters became common, replacing crumbling fireplaces or rusty Warm Morning stoves and vastly improving the smell of the towns. On winter mornings on Greasy Creek, the cloud of gray-brown smoke that perpetually floated overhead gradually vanished, giving eyelashes and nostrils a reprieve from the grit that used to settle from the acrid fog. The ancient fire that burned above the town in the slate dump, a refuse pile where the unsalable product of the coal seams was discarded, finally burned out after decades of smoldering.

Some of the houses fell into such disrepair that it was necessary to remove them. Sometimes mobile homes began to appear on the empty lots, heralding a flood of cheap shelter later on. Some lots that were not occupied had gardens planted within them, but many spaces lay abandoned. The chimney foundations that remained stood like unfinished tombstones that bespoke no testament to the dramas played out there, and the empty ground grew up in briars, where children competed with birds for the gooseberries or blackberries that burst out in those tangled spots.

Eventually, only the barest outline of the town of Greasy Creek remained, like the fossil of some prehistoric beast. Today, only seven houses bear witness to the fact that a great company town lived in that narrow valley; a hundred others are gone, sold at a fraction of the cost of construction to anyone who could afford one. But even that is remarkable; many old towns have no original structures left at all. Unlike the ghost towns of the far West, where the residents disappeared after the gold seams worked out or the water dried up, in the hills the people remained. Their houses, which they never owned anyway, vanished instead.

Most of the public buildings on Greasy Creek fell before I was born. The church was carefully dismantled and re-erected in Pikeville during World War II, when building materials were scarce and the need for prayer was great. The walls of the old church still house the faithful, but hear few entreaties for the souls of the recently maimed or killed in the pits, since relatively few real miners are at work in Pike County now. More commonly, men blast the mountains into submission and haul away the coal like thieves absconding with their loot.

The tiny hospital that was scarcely bigger than a private home by today's standards finally became one, and the Greasy Creek Hotel, where visitors and unmarried supervisors of the company boarded, became a post office and general store. The new owners closed the upstairs rooms, where more than one naïve valley belle met a mine boss or passing drummer in the vain hope of leaving the town as a wealthy bride. The brick bathhouse, because it could not be dismantled, remained empty for years, going through incarnations as a church, a pharmacy, and then a shell again. Halloween pranksters eventually burned it out, leaving only sturdy brick walls that were bulldozed down.

This heartless disassembly partly explains why I never considered Greasy Creek a town, and applied to most of my fellow pilgrims in 1967. We never considered any of our vanished camps to be real towns. We never knew them as prosperous and busy, never knew the swagger of streets crowded with people, never heard accents of workers from other countries who came there to make their fortunes. We never saw company baseball teams in actions, never watched well-dressed supervisors and their ladies enter hotels for cotillions, and never heard our own brass bands play patriotic music on the Fourth of July. When we passed through what was left of those weary places on our daily rides to high school, we did not think of the stories that could have been told, and could not, or would not, acknowledge the forlorn spirits evicted from them, ghosts that drifted above the abandoned chimneys or through the silent streets, bewildered at having no place to haunt, until they too gave up and departed.

Although other towns lived longer than Greasy Creek, they all died a tortured death, with no one able to restrain their passing. There was no debate and no calls from the citizenry to continue; no mayors or city councils to lobby; no town halls; and no debates over utility rates. There had been policemen who maintained order and shined their badges like real police officers, but they were not public servants. There were sometimes courts and judges, but they dispensed justice only to the extent that it affected the fortunes of the companies. When the mines worked out or the coal was no longer needed, this artificial governance disappeared, like many of the immigrants who moved away, back to the old country or to other towns where there was still work, and where they would enter nearly identical pits, under the very earth where their bodies would eventually be consigned.

As for me, and most of my generation, we had no compassion for this loss. We had not seen our towns created, had not lived in them during the heady days of their existence, and we had nothing to mourn for. By the time we went to high school, we had learned that no matter how much coal was mined under our mountains, we would glean no wealth from it as our ancestors had signed away all rights before even our grandparents were born. The true impact of that travesty was not felt for a hundred years, but we had learned that we were little more than squatters on our own land and we were disenchanted. We had learned there was an alternative, another world away from the hills, a world that had nothing to do with slate dumps and coal dust and sorrow.

Although we might not have been able to articulate our longing, we yearned for something else. We wanted a new pilgrimage, and even in the deepest coves, we heard exotic music, siren calls to mythical places where we could be free and live our lives in a new age that was dawning. There was California with its deeply tanned women and endless beaches on the other side of the country; Colorado, where mountains parted clouds that would never graze our Appalachians; or Mexico, where Carlos Castenada promised us an even more mystical experience. We promised ourselves that we would not become coal miners like our fathers; that we would not die in darkness under mountains we played on as children.

We may not have known there was a Summer of Love somewhere outside the camps, but we knew there was more to life than what we knew. We left to find work, but we yearned for adventure, for experience, for knowledge; hillbillies or not, we knew there had to be something more than the benighted towns we came from, and when school was done we streamed like lemmings to Cleveland or Chicago or Detroit, anywhere to get away.

In the end, however, few of us really went very far, and we mostly traded the dangerous monotony of coal field life for the numbing regimentation of northern cities, where we worked in the same factories our fathers worked when they left the hills. We rarely looked back as we departed and usually ignored the warnings we were given as we packed our trunks and said our good-byes.

That was why I left Greasy Creek. Two years after I came back from Ohio, still unsatisfied, I left again. This time I went east, but even in Virginia, the Colony from which my family had come nearly two hundred years ago, something called me home. Now I find myself admitting what I always denied; that it truly was home, that there is something different about these primal hills, these worn ridges, the world's oldest and the most haunted. Others have felt it too, this unexplained longing for a place we never really knew.

I saw it in the eyes of my expatriate families in the North; I saw it in the faces of the mountain boys I worked with there. I have seen it even amid the neon glow of Las Vegas, where I once sat down at a blackjack table and recognized a familiar melody in the speech of a table-mate. We share that, all of us, and I suspect at one time in our lives all of us wanted nothing more than to get away as fast and as far as we could.

Yet in our retreat, in our Diaspora, we would sometimes be visited by dreams of our lost cities of the hills, and sometimes dreams of what they were before they were built, before steel and coal came marching into our souls; odd dreams, dreams that were kinder than the images we used to justify our flights.

And we would sometimes wake up startled, in the middle of the night, wondering where the visions came from.

Household Gods

People would come and go all day at the Perry-Payne Building on Superior Avenue in Cleveland, scurrying to the offices of the great steel and coal firms that occupied the structure. Engineers, land agents, lawyers, clerks, job seekers and other sycophants regularly walked through the eight-story atrium, occasionally stopping to admire the grand murals that dominated the lobby and then moving on to their appointments. The building had been the pride of Cleveland when it was built and was still more popular than the larger Standard Oil Building nearby, perhaps because Clevelanders disliked both the owner of the latter structure and its stark architecture.

On an early November day in 1913, the interior lights in Perry-Payne had been turned on early, since ominous clouds gathering above Lake Erie had restricted the usual flood of sunlight that filled the atrium. In the crowd, sparser than normal because of the approaching storm, no one would have paid particular attention to a group of four young men hurriedly making their way. Snowflakes had appeared on their hats as they walked down Superior Avenue and had noticeably picked up speed as they opened the imposing front doors.

The atmosphere, both inside and outside Perry-Payne, matched the mood of the young men.

"I worry about this meeting," one of them muttered, almost to himself. "I very much worry about this meeting."

The group had just returned from a long journey and submitted a final report on their activities to the president of the firm whose offices they were now approaching. For the better part of a year, they had traipsed around Kentucky, West Virginia, Virginia and part of Tennessee on assignment from Price McKinney, President and Chief Executive Officer of Corrigan, McKinney and Company. They had done their work, followed their instructions, and completed their mission.

Now all of them wondered if they would be fired for what they did.

"I know what you mean," another one said. "I do not relish being cast out into the streets."

"I don't think we should fear anything," said yet another, although with little conviction. "I think Mr. McKinney should be impressed with our work."

"That I do not doubt," the first one replied. "But impressed by what? Our diligence or our audacity?"

Although their nervousness had not abated, the men fell silent when they walked into the outer office and were directed to the desk of the assistant to the president. When the men announced their presence, the assistant did not speak, but merely took out and opened his gold pocket watch, looked at the men, and closed it with an audible click before retiring to McKinney's private office.

"Criminy!" one of the men said. "We're doomed."

Somewhere behind that heavy, deeply polished wooden door, their fates were being sealed. In fact, McKinney was making a final scan of the pages of the report when his assistant walked in.

Price McKinney was one of the industrial titans of Cleveland and was already somewhat of a legend. He had taken a broken, bankrupt pig iron company and, phoenix-like, raised it from its ashes to become one of the most energetic steel corporations on the shores of the Great Lakes. Corrigan, McKinney and Company had its genesis in the demise of a previous firm, Corrigan and Ives, and twenty years later, the circumstances of that death and rebirth were still being talked about.

Corrigan and Ives itself had been born of another company, but under more auspicious circumstances and of a different mother than steel. Most of the capital for Corrigan and Ives came from oil.

The two largest stockholders in Corrigan and Ives were James W. Corrigan, popularly referred to as "Captain Jim," since his first fortune had been made in hauling iron ore from Minnesota to Cleveland in his fleet of boats, and Franklin Rockefeller, who had shares in Standard Oil and was a brother to John Davison and William, who owned most of the company.

Captain Jim owned a crude oil refinery and a patent for refining oil that was far more efficient than John D's and the great robber baron wanted both. Although Captain Jim was willing to sell, John D did not want to pay his price and attempted to squeeze the smaller company into submission by cutting the price of his products. It was Rockefeller's most effective technique, but it did not work on Corrigan, since he could match each cut and still make money. John D was eventually forced to acquiesce and Captain Jim saw an opportunity in steel as a place to invest the money he made. He personally bought some of the ore lands he had been shipping from and took a note on a larger tract along with Frank Rockefeller and formed Corrigan and Ives. The misfortune of the two men was that they had borrowed the money from John D.

In 1893, a financial panic plunged the country into depression and Corrigan and Ives, which had been making money, suddenly found itself in arrears to its creditors. John D, who could easily have waited for the economy to improve, decided to call in the note. He would have his revenge on Captain Jim, and if his brother would suffer in the process, so be it; business was business.

Both men were financially devastated, but not completely ruined. For another five years, Frank would continue to work for

Standard Oil, but would rarely speak to his brother. In 1898, he left the company and, after a final falling out, never spoke to John D again, despite both his brothers' entreaties. He died in 1917 after leaving instructions that he was not to be buried in the Rockefeller family plot. He might have been unlucky, for he had lost much in business, in contrast to his brothers and especially John D, but he found some success in another Ohio foundry, which he turned over to the father and grandfather of two men who became presidents of the United States.

Judge Stevenson Burke, a respected Ohio jurist, was assigned the receivership of Corrigan and Ives, and brought in a young accountant from Toledo to parcel out the corpse of the dead company. He had heard of Price McKinney and thought he saw enough in the remains of Captain Jim's company for McKinney to salvage. In 1894, some twenty years before the four young men tenuously walked into McKinney's office, the firm of Corrigan, McKinney and Company was born. Forty percent of the company belonged to Captain Jim, since most of the assets came from him; thirty percent of the company belonged to Price McKinney, since he had saved most of the former from auction, and most of the "and Company" belonged to Judge Burke, since it was his reputation that helped secure the notes for working capital. Soon those notes were repaid, and Corrigan-McKinney began expanding.

That was the reason for McKinney's dispatch of his team to Kentucky: he wanted a fully integrated company. The term "integrated" referred only to business in 1913; it had nothing to do with racial issues, although McKinney was very much an adherent to the tenets of the Progressive Era. The Civil Rights movement was a half-century away, and had McKinney lived then, he might have been an advocate, but now his major issue was securing all the raw materials to make steel. He used as a model Henry Ford, who was building at River Rouge in Michigan an industrial complex the likes of which the world had never seen. In one location, all the raw materials, steel, glass, leather, and wood came together to produce a finished product. McKinney already had his iron ore fields, but his only coal mine, in Pennsylvania, was nearing depletion. In order to have the same security for Corrigan-McKinney, he needed coal lands of his own and he needed them now; his new steel mill would soon be completed and hungry.

During his frequent trips to Lexington, Kentucky, where he occasionally bought horses for Wickliffe Stables, his horse farm outside Cleveland, he was told of the rapid development of coal fields in Eastern Kentucky. He heard the coal was hot, cheap, and, with the penetration of railroads into the mountains, easy to ship. McKinney also saw an opportunity to practice the humanism he preached: he would build a model town where the workers would be treated decently and would produce efficiently.

He had already applied that theory to Corrigan, McKinney and Company; his pay scale was generous and he gave bonuses. One time the bonus he paid his men equaled their yearly wages. He encouraged clean living and provided recreational opportunities for his workers. During the summer, one of his favorite pastimes was sitting in the bleachers, urging on his company baseball team as they scored runs over the players from his friendly rival Otis Steel.

The four young men now waited outside the office with rapidly beating hearts. Although they did not know it, their report confirmed exactly what McKinney had anticipated. He nodded to his aide, who left the room and returned with the men in tow. McKinney suppressed a smile when he noticed their knees were shaking. He bade them approach and be seated.

"Gentlemen, I have been reviewing your findings," McKinney began. "And it would appear that you have obligated this company to a considerable expense should we exercise these options." His brow knitted as he looked at the ceiling high above the young men. "I do not recall authorizing such a large commitment."

"Sir," said one of the men, assuming the role of spokesman. "We realize the options we secured were more than we antici-pated, but we felt it prudent to do so."

"Prudent?" McKinney interrupted. "Acquiring such large tracts would imply just the opposite. Why would we need so much coal?"

The young man could almost see a spectral hand writing with an ancient quill across the wall behind the man with round, thick glasses in front of him, a man with absolute power to fire him at any time. He chose his words carefully.

"Sir, we were of the impression that the Company would continue to expand and, in addition to filling our current needs, we would have ample reserves for the future." His strategy was a gamble, but he had to take it. "As you most certainly have noted, the cost of the properties we would acquire is far below what we anticipated."

"These mineral analyses," McKinney said, picking up one of the pages in front of him. "Are you confident of their accuracy?"

"Yes, sir. The thermal value of this coal is unbelievably high." The young man felt he might be making progress; his confidence rose. "Its coking ability is superb."

"And why would we need two operations to secure it?"

The man's confidence fell just as rapidly. The strategy he used before, invoking the philosophy of Price McKinney to justify his actions, would have to be used again.

"Sir, the reason we are planning our own coal operations is to ensure a secure supply of coal. If we have only one mine, there is the possibility of an interruption in our supply if some-thing happens to that mine."

"But what would prevent us from having multiple portals?"

"Nothing, sir, and that is in our plans. However, should we have some other problem, labor issues or the like, it would be wise to have an alternative location some distance away to confine any such problems to their origin."

McKinney scratched his chin and appeared to be considering the young man's arguments. He decided to string him along just a while longer.

"Local agents?" he inquired.

"Sir, we have several candidates and our first recommendation is a Mr. Icuabud Sanders, known as 'IB' locally. He was very helpful to us in finding the leases we desired."

"This 'Greasy Creek' location—am I given to believe we would have to build our own railroad to it? I note that the other location ..." McKinney pulled out a map. "Er ... Wolfpit. An intriguing name. I see it has an existing railroad that would travel through the center of camp. Why should we invest in building a new railroad if rails already exist?"

"Well, there are few other suitable locations on the rails, which largely follow the river throughout Pike County. And there actually is a rail bed into Greasy Creek, although it is narrow gauge. It was used some twenty years ago by the Yellow Poplar Lumber Company of Ironton, Ohio for timbering purposes. It would not be that expensive to bring it up to modern standards.

"This Mr. Sanders, what else do you have to recommend him?"

The young man relaxed a bit and went on; he was very confident on this matter.

"Mr. Sanders is well-read and surprisingly articulate. He and his wife make an interesting couple. Both are children of Confederate soldiers, although she is much more the partisan of the two, yet we found no one on Greasy Creek who would not recommend him, regardless of family loyalties, which are very strong in this region. Many families were entirely riven by the Civil War in that area. We did not know how intrusive the conflict was until we visited."

McKinney said nothing and the young man continued: "Mrs. Sanders made it a point to inform us that she was quite proud of the fact that her father was one of the final guards of Confederate President Jefferson Davis in his ill-fated flight when the War ended."

"The Sanders live on Greasy Creek?"

"Yes, sir."

McKinney took off his glasses, extracted a pristine white handkerchief from his pocket and began wiping his lenses as he slowly shook his head. He took a deep breath and released an audible sigh. The most frightened of the young men before him was mentally preparing a telegram to his father, asking for money for passage home, when McKinney spoke.

"Gentlemen, I see no reason to continue this conversation. There is simply no alternative but to require you to return to Kentucky post haste and execute all these options."

The men felt the sword drop, but realized it had not yet reached their necks when McKinney spoke again: "I repeat, *all* these options. In addition, I will expect you to locate any additional tracts as may be available adjoining these or elsewhere."

Wait a minute, one of them thought, are we not fired?

"Gentlemen, congratulations on excellent work." Price McKinney came smiling from behind his desk with hand extended. The men were slack-jawed as the president of Corrigan, McKinney and Company in turn took each of their right hands in a firm grip. "Your contribution to the future success of this company will be noted."

McKinney's assistant eased silently up to the group and stood waiting for the men to be dismissed. Practically all were in a daze as the full realization of what had just happened began to sink in. McKinney spoke one last time as they began to walk away.

"Gentlemen, one last thing: when you return to Kentucky, please extend my compliments to Mr. and Mrs. Sanders. Tell them I should very much like to call on them when I visit."

After the men left, McKinney sat down in his chair and turned to the window, looking out at the storm now beginning to pound the windowpanes. It was dark and foreboding, but he saw brightness there, or at least could imagine it. He saw the glow of his mill illuminating the night sky, Kentucky coal blazing, Minnesota ore smelting, the slag swept away and white-hot ingots of steel rolling. For twenty years, he had anticipated this moment and now he wanted to savor it.

Presently, he turned to more personal issues. Specifically, he was in the market for a new home. He knew his current residence in Cleveland was insufficient for the social activities he would soon have to endure. He loved his horse farm and preferred living there to anywhere, but his wife enjoyed entertaining, far more than he, in fact, and it was time to consider a new home, something more appropriate.

On East Boulevard, he had watched a grand mansion rise and was impressed by its restrained style; he did not appreciate anything overly ornate. It had been commissioned by the widow of Abraham Lincoln's confidante John Hay, whom McKinney very much admired, and it had been designed by Abram Garfield, son of the late President James A. Garfield, whom he admired even more. But the mansion had remained empty for two years now, and he began to suspect Mrs. Hay might never live there. She might be willing to sell, he thought.

It had been a successful day and he was cheered, in spite of the threatening weather. Price McKinney did not know the Great Lakes Storm of 1913 was bearing down on Cleveland at that moment, but even if he had, he would not have worried. Clevelanders had never experienced the fury of a November gale like what was now approaching, and no one would ever see such a storm again. When it was over, the city was buried under two feet of ice and snow and without power for days. Ships sank across the Great Lakes and newspapers estimated 273 people had died, but McKinney would not have changed his schedule if he could have seen into the future. He was happiest when he was working, so in spite of the wind howling at his windows, he turned back to his desk and began again.

On Greasy Creek, the weather had also closed in. The previous summer had been a good one and most everyone was prepared for winter. Cellars and pits were full of root vegetables and shuck beans and onions hung happily from walls and porch beams. Jars and tubs of kraut and beets and beans were sealed or covered and stored away for use in the winter and the men who had jobs had saved enough to buy warm coats for their children. Except for new money, which eased so many mothers' minds, things had not changed much in the hills in a hundred years. The War and its aftermath had taken a fearful toll, but things were different now: real jobs were appearing and there was a rumor going round that even Greasy Creek might soon have work. The winter did not threaten the people so much anymore; children were already looking ahead to Christmas and the smell of pine trees in the house.

No one on Greasy Creek knew what had just transpired in Cleveland, except perhaps IB Sanders, and no one knew the devastation soon to strike that faraway city. But IB would not have known the storm that was soon to be loosed upon Greasy Creek. On winter nights, he liked to read by the fireplace and he might have had a copy of Yeats to peruse that night, and he may have wondered what awesome, rough beast now slouched unstoppably toward Greasy Creek, impatiently waiting to be born.

*   *   *

On a cold November day, fifty years after Price McKinney accepted his engineers' report, I was half-asleep, riding my school bus home when the bus driver slowed to pick up an adult male passenger. The weather was not overly miserable, but Ed Ratliff, a distant cousin and close friend of my father, appreciated the gesture. He got on the bus carrying two large bags of groceries and sat down behind me.

"Stockin' up for winter, Ed?" I asked.

He smiled in response.

We made small talk and he asked me the usual questions about family until we passed through the camps. Ed looked out the window and sighed. On the roof of yet another of the few remaining camp houses, workers were tearing away great strips of tarpaper and dropping them to the ground. The windows of the old house had been removed, and other workers were tossing out boards and ragged pieces of wood. Yet another worker was feeding a large fire with the debris. Black smoke curled around the doomed house as if it were a febrile spirit in a last attempt to protect the body it had just departed.

"Well, there goes another one," he said. "Bruce, do you ever wonder what happened here, why this town shut down?"

"No," I said honestly. "I figured they ran out of coal."

"No, that wasn't it. There was all kinds of coal here, still is; best coal in the United States."

That surprised me. Why would the town shut down if the mine hadn't worked out? Pike County had, and still has, only one real industry: coal mining. The opening and closing of coal mines occurred regularly as boundaries played out. I thought Greasy Creek's coal was gone and the hills were vast hollow shells.

My ears perked up.

Ed took another deep breath. We had passed the camp and were now heading up the main Greasy Creek road. He began a tale I believed but could not confirm for nearly forty years. He said the management had idled the mine because the company had lost its leadership with the death of the last male stockholder. Now only four widows were responsible for the vast operation and the decision was made to sell it.

It was a shock, he said, when orders came down from Cleveland to suspend operations, but everyone thought it would be temporary. Everything had been left in place and it was logical to assume that the mine would surely reopen when a new owner bought it. But a year later, the stock market crashed, the De-

tled in and there was no need for Greasy Creek's
5, the sale was made, but it was four years before
s done with the mine or the camps. At that time, the
steel business had picked up with orders for material for another world war, but an engineering team sent to assess the
possibility of reopening found that the mine had been never
been properly mothballed and was now too dangerous to
reopen, even by Kentucky's minimal standards. Since the coal
could be reached from other locations, the portals were ordered
sealed, the houses sold or torn down to escape taxes, and the
steel underpinnings of the entire operation were taken away for
scrap.

Greasy Creek's fate was a harbinger of things to come for all
the coal towns. Some of them survived during the Second World
War, but only because of it. Within a decade, the era was over as
coal seams played out or companies were hit by recessions
during the Fifties. From the Depression onward, there was
always more men than work, and no need for Greasy Creek's
new owner or any of the companies to maintain towns they had
built all over the Appalachians. In those forlorn places, the
death spasms began or accelerated when the war ended, and by
the time the first Beatle song was played on our transistor
radios, the towns were gone, along with the hope of their residents. Annual high school graduations produced a flood tide of
job seekers during the Sixties and few found work at home.

Ed could sense that I would have left Greasy Creek even if
there had been work, but he wanted to know what I would be
leaving.

"You ought to talk to your Paw Pete," Ed told me. "He practically built this town, you know. He ran the construction
crews."

"Paw Pete did?" I was amazed; that was something I did not
know. Paw Pete was Peter Prater, my great-grandfather on my
mother's side of the family. He was a happy, gregarious, and
vigorous man, surprisingly youthful in demeanor. His mother

was Granny Malissy Prater, "Aunt" Malissy to everyone else on Greasy Creek, as the custom was to address all elderly souls as Aunt or Uncle. She led a long life; dying at 97 in 1953, not long after my seventh birthday.

The previous spring, she was sprightly enough to hide Easter eggs for my siblings and me at my grandfather Andrew Prater's house. I did not realize it at the time, but I am fond of revealing this fact now: I actually touched someone who lived through the Civil War; someone who was alive when Lee was in the field, when Lincoln paced with ghosts through the White House. I knew someone who saw her father come home a broken, weary soldier in gray after watching his country die.

When Malissa's son died nearly thirty years later, his obituary said he was 101. When I researched my family, I found that Peter Prater was actually 102. The Praters usually lived long lives. By contrast, my Hopkins family members rarely escaped their seventies.

At Sunday dinners at any of my three grandmothers' houses, it was not unusual to see Peter seated at the head of the table as guest of honor. Once at Rissie's house, I noticed how steady and strong he was, while my grandfather Frank Hopkins's hands would shake while raising his coffee cup to his lips. Frank was a generation younger, but then I did not know the reason for his trembling. Peter was an honored guest at any house and when asked he would preside over the table with a regal decorum, but I would never have imagined him in his youth. I could not imagine any of my elders in their youth.

As a child I was too young to realize that everyone goes through the same stages of life. Every week I would watch the two popular TV medical dramas on our black-and-white screen: *Dr. Kildare* and *Ben Casey, MD*. In the latter, the same introduction began every program as a pedagogical hand would appear and draw symbols on a blackboard while intoning the words: *man...woman...birth...death...infinity*. It was a grim assessment, and by the Sixties I was determined such a predictable fate would not be mine.

Nevertheless, Ed's words intrigued me.

"Paw Pete actually built the camps?" I asked again, feeling an unfamiliar surge of pride. I was Peter Prater's first great-grandson.

"Yup, and another one of your people was an important man in the company. IB Sanders was an agent for McKinney Steel."

I had heard the name, but IB died years before I was born; so had his wife Adelaide. My mother told me her mother would often dispatch her to stay all night with Aunt Adelaide, who would often startle guests by rising suddenly from her chair, breaking wind quite loudly for a tiny woman, and then sitting back down to resume the conversation at the mid-sentence point she abandoned it.

"In fact, when old man McKinney came to Greasy Creek," Ed added. "He stayed with IB and Adelaide. He did that two or three times."

"Who was old man McKinney?" I asked.

"McKinney Steel. He owned the company."

I had to wonder if Aunt Adelaide would have restrained herself during his visits.

"Your family had a lot to do with the camps, Bruce. They asked your great-grandpaw Luke Hamlin to run the commissary, but they never did build it. Just the foundation."

"Where was the commissary?"

"That big, old concrete foundation in the lower end of the camps, where all the frogs are."

I knew it well; we often gigged its inhabitants with long poles from its walls. On summer evenings there would be a deafening hallelujah chorus emanating from the protected swamp they ruled.

"Your Paw Pete probably remembers better than anybody what it was like here, before the mines came, too," Ed continued. "Him and your Mamaw Rissie know just about everything there is to know about Greasy Creek, especially since Aunt Malissy died. The only person who knew more was Mammy, your great-great grandmother Dorcus."

That I knew well; for years Rissie, who lived squarely in the middle of the old town, had told me stories of my family, mostly of the Hopkins and Praters. Some of the stories took place long before she was born and were told to her by Dorcus, who was her own grandmother. The stories were about the Old Ones—the first settlers on Greasy Creek, the Civil War, its awful aftermath, and the people in my family who lived then.

She told me of my ancestors, including Elisha Hopkins, who had four wives, made whiskey, had Indians as his closest friends, and tried to keep his family out of war. She told me about Elisha's son George, who was a Union soldier and married his first cousin Victoria, who was the daughter of a Confederate soldier, Elisha's brother Joseph. She told me of the tragedy of her death three days after their marriage. She told me about so many others: Praters, Phillipses, Hamlins; people whom I could never have known, but whose stories I needed to remember because they were my people. I was entranced as she told stories of the War itself, stories I had somehow failed to associate with the accounts I read in the history books.

And she told me about her own life—how she had taken my father as a dying child from her brother who had lost his wife and first son and nearly lost his mind. She was given the task of saving him and raising him as her own and she did both magnificently.

"Aunt Rissie led some kind of life," Ed told me. He used 'Aunt,' the affectionate term for a female elder, even though she was not his aunt. I was accustomed to hearing it and understood. Ed also understood that Rissie was my grandmother in every way but by birth.

Perhaps he knew that I was tending away from the past, that the remains of the old coal town held no charm for me, that I would flee Pike County as soon as I could, and he was reminding me of the importance of my elders and the opportunity I was squandering by not spending more time with them. He knew that I would not have gainsaid my grandmother for anything, but he could also sense I was beginning to discount the stories that held me spellbound as a child, that I was filing them away, like grade school stories a high school student no longer reads. And it did seem that the people she told me about were as detached from the Greasy Creek I knew as the stories I was reading then of life on Mars.

I could relate somewhat to tales about the old people I knew, those whom I could see shuffling into church or from house to house, but the Old Ones were no more real to me than Ray Bradbury's Martians. Instead of challenging her stories, which would have been heartless, I let them slip from my memory, just as the old camp houses of Greasy Creek were slipping away.

But Ed had ignited a new interest in the town and its people in me.

The bus slowed as it approached his house and he gathered his bags. Before he disembarked, he looked squarely into my eyes and spoke: "You need to talk to your family, Bruce. Listen to Rissie and Paw Pete. Ask them questions; write it down."

He searched my face to see if I was listening.

I was. I truly was.

"You'll regret it one of these days if you don't," he said in a final admonition. He searched my face and seemed satisfied that he had reached me.

Indeed he had. That night, I promised myself that I would spend more time with my elders, that I would seek out those stories and save them from the inconsequential fate of the old town on Greasy Creek.

Ed's words indeed had an effect, and that night I dreamed. Faces began to materialize in my dream; answers to old questions began to be revealed. I could smell honeysuckle, even though it was November.

The next day, John Kennedy was shot dead in Dallas. I forgot all my promises and would not come back to them for nearly forty years.

*   *   *

In the early spring of 1916, word passed rapidly that a strange troop of men had just gotten off the train at Ward siding, which was built on flat land beside the Big Sandy for the Yellow Poplar Lumber Company. The company stacked logs there after they were brought out of Greasy Creek by a tiny engine that struggled with its mighty cargo When the spring floods came, the logs were rolled into the water like armless corpses. Some said the engine puffed as hard going up Greasy Creek as coming down, but it played its role in denuding most of the hillsides that once graced the valley with unmatched shade, even in the hottest summer. In spite of its service, when the trees were gone the little engine was summarily cut into scrap and hauled away on a steamboat. Now its larger brethren would return to Greasy Creek and these men would prepare its roadway.

This group of men frightened the people of Greasy Creek because they were nearly coal black. Pike County had its Negroes, descendants of the small number of slaves that lived there and died in bondage before Emancipation, but their color had been diluted by generations of miscegenation. They were the result of slave owners increasing their wealth by incorporating their own genes into their breeding stock or by taking what comfort they could from their human possessions, who had no right to refuse.

After the men had gotten off and set up camp, more trains appeared with huge, noisy machines that resounded all the way to the head of the creek: steam shovels and steam hammers that groaned and chattered and hooted and whistled until they reached the forks of Greasy Creek where, their mission complete, they were loaded onto the bright new rails that had almost magically appeared as the crew advanced. For the most part, Greasy Creek left these alien beings alone, although enough contact was made to allow some of their stories to be told.

They were from Virginia, not the mountains that bordered Pike County, but much farther east, in the flatlands near the ocean, where generations of their ancestors had lived and died as chattels of other people, within sight of the water that carried their unremembered fathers away from freedom. When their job was finished, they struck their tents, boarded another train, and disappeared, leaving the residents of Greasy Creek to wonder what was coming next. Price McKinney, pleased with their work, ordered bonuses to be paid.

That summer, McKinney spent a night with IB and Adelaide and revealed to IB his plans for the model town he was building to support the great mine that had just opened. He trusted them, although he recognized immediately that Adelaide's Confederate patriotism was far more immediate that IB's. But like friends and family who visited, they shared stories around IB's fireplace. Inevitably, they spoke of the War, but in deference to Adelaide, McKinney did not share his deep respect for an Ohio colonel who was sworn in as a Brigadier General on President Lincoln's direct orders in Pikeville. Instead, they talked more about the future than the past.

McKinney did tell them about his eighteen years in Mexico, where he mined gold, and he told them the story of Corrigan, McKinney and Company, whose name he would soon abbreviate to the McKinney Steel Company. He would do so with no imperial pretensions; he was simply the only male owner left in the company and his partners would have wanted it this way. He told them how from merely a business relationship with Captain Jim Corrigan, a true friendship had grown. When almost all of Captain Jim's family drowned in a yachting tragedy on Lake Erie, the Captain was too grief-stricken to find a place to bury them. He turned to McKinney, who selected the cemetery and the spot, and bought the adjoining plot for his own family.

Captain Jim died eight years later and both he and the other deceased partner had given almost total control of the company to McKinney on their passing. He probably did not tell them the only heir of Captain Jim had recently married and practically no one in Cleveland accepted an invitation to the wedding or would have anything to do with the couple, because he may have considered that information uninteresting to his hosts.

He proudly told them of his plans: how Greasy Creek would be the most modern camp in the coal fields; that the ponies the miners were using would soon be replaced with electric engines. He loved horses and would not use these animals a minute longer than necessary. He explained that the chute that had been built to direct coal into waiting cars would be replaced with the most technologically advanced system to move coal on the planet. He said his miners would have decent houses, and good doctors to treat the men and their families, and brand-new electric lamps to work by, instead of the hopelessly weak coal-oil lamps that cast little more light than a winter sunset. He told them he wanted nothing more from his employees than a good day's work for a good day's pay. When Price McKinney boarded his private coach to leave, he shook hands with a new friend. By then, the two men on that uncompleted dock deeply respected each other.

When McKinney returned to Cleveland, he moved into the mansion he had wanted since the first day he saw it rising, and hosted the obligatory housewarming ball to welcome the rest of Cleveland's Main Line.

He did not invite the son of his former partner.

Before he left, he dispatched IB to the Illinois Basin coal field in Western Kentucky to find more miners, carpenters, masons, clerks and skilled tradesmen to build the town of Greasy Creek. The coal towns of Western Kentucky would not need them, as the coal now being produced in the east would soon overtake the market. A ton of Pike County coal would burn hotter and longer than two from Muhlenberg or Ohio counties, and their workers would be happy to come where the work was plentiful and wages were higher.

He gave IB a copy of a book published the previous year, a book he much enjoyed and thought IB might want to read on the train. It was about the Illinois Basin, or at least part of it, and its success enabled an idealistic young lawyer, who barely made a living defending the poor, to concentrate on writing. Indeed, the book became an American classic, but the poet never again achieved the success of that one unmatched moment of his life.

One of the poems was about a hapless Negro, a foil of the yahoos of the town, a gullible, hardworking blacksmith who was tricked unmercifully, but was much more attune than they to the unseen world around him. In spite of his tribulations, he harbored no ill will for his tormentors and sought no revenge for the injuries they inflicted on him.

And he was wise when he said they "didn't know any more than the horseshoes did what moved [them] about Spoon River."

April 1917

*A*lthough Pikeville was proud of its bridge, many more horses crossed it than automobiles, which were still rare in Pike County. A few wealthy merchants or coal barons had a Reo or a Dodge, but like the rest of the country, Fords were most popular for those who could afford a car. Yet, anyone crossing the bridge would face little oncoming traffic due to the scarcity of such machines and the fact that no horseback rider would take a chance on his mount bolting if it faced a huffing, smoking mechanical beast on the narrow floor of the huge structure.

The bridge was solid steel and not yet ten years old, and was built just downstream from the Chloe Creek landing, where a ferry had crossed from one side of the river to the other for over a century, and steamboats had tied up for more than half that time. The bridge was built high on the mountainside across from Pikeville to allow room for the steamers to pass under, accommodating a favorite pastime of the young boys of the town: tossing corncobs into smokestacks as the boats sloshed toward the dock. Still, the town was changing and the spoke factory, once limited to making replacements for the worn and broken wheels on the wagons of Pike County farmers, was now producing automobile wheels as well. Business was good: the roads of Pike County, what there were, were not easily subdued.

On this day however, there was much more traffic than normal, especially for Easter, as flivvers puffed up and down Pikeville's streets and across the bridge. Some horsemen were impatient enough to chance the passage as an auto approached from the other side. The horses may have sensed their riders' urgency or they may have simply acquiesced in their owners' demands, but they went forward and galloped by the snorting beasts. There was a much-increased haste in everyone's manner today, and a crowd had gathered at the telegraph office, which had not closed since Friday because of the volume of messages it was receiving.

On Greasy Creek, this Easter was little different from any other; the incessant hammering in the camps was temporarily stilled as the workmen discarded their tools to spend Sunday with their families and in church. The Greasy Creek Old Regular Baptist Church sat empty, however, as its membership attended services in Little Creek, just across the mountain, where one of the founders of the Greasy Creek Church, the old Civil War soldier Robert Damron, had spoken mightily to the assemblage of his circuit and allowed himself a well-deserved sip of "medicine" after he sat down. By late afternoon, after countless Easter dinners on Greasy Creek and Little Creek and Shelby Creek and all the creeks draining into the Big Sandy, the guests said their goodbyes and began their journeys home, stopping along the way to pay their respects to other families and perhaps share a final piece of custard pie with a venerable aunt or uncle.

At Harmon Robinson's house, where Harrison's family often shared Easter since Mammy, the last true Hopkins matriarch, had been laid to rest four years before, the afternoon was progressing slowly and heads were nodding in submission to the chicken and dumplings and deviled eggs that had disappeared from Harmon's table. Talk had turned for a while, as it usually did, to the past and to Elisha, the omnipresent ghost of the Hopkins clan, regardless of whether they were

Hopkinses, Robinsons or Blackburns, but the past soon yielded to the present, or more properly the future. For the most part, the talk was of new jobs and new money infusing the families of Greasy Creek. Indeed, Harmon's great two-story house was barely four years old and had been a gift from a son who profited handsomely from selling his land to the company. With a real town rising on Greasy Creek, the old days seemed less and less relevant, especially to the young people, for legends can be easily forgotten when the past collides with the future.

Rissie Hopkins, whose stories of those legends could not compete in such a heady atmosphere, put on the new coat her mother had bought her and buttoned it. With work so plentiful, there were many new coats this Easter, even though the usually still-chilly spring had warmed considerably. Rissie announced her intention to make her way across the field to Melissa Prater's house.

"You want me to go with you, Sissy?" Bessie Hopkins, Rissie's younger sister inquired.

"No, I'm just going to step over to Aunt Malissy's," Rissie replied. "You can stay here if you want." It took little persuasion for Bessie to remain at Harmon's. She had been smitten with Harmon's son John since she first saw him. Bessie would be nine years old this month and John would turn fourteen in June, but the families knew that eventually they would marry. Everyone agreed the two children were made for each other.

Everyone also agreed there would soon be a wedding for Rissie's older brother Frank, who had only perfunctorily supped with the Robinsons, and made his hurried exit to walk on up the main Greasy Creek road. He was on his way to the home of Paris Coleman, where Paris's daughter Manie Ethel had been attempting to disguise her anxious glances out the window in anticipation of Frank's arrival. Both of Harrison's older sons were of marriageable age and his oldest daughter was already wed. The family knew Frank would be next, and he endured the usual teasing from siblings and cousins as he dashed outside after given leave by his father.

After Rissie left, the members of the family exchanged their usual sad glances with each other, as they knew it would be unlikely that Rissie would ever be so lucky. They were grateful, however, that Rissie found a friend in Aunt Malissy, since the loss of Mammy was still quick.

As Rissie crossed the bridge to Malissa's house, she could hear music from the front porch and took notice of a strikingly handsome black-haired boy, just past his eleventh birthday, plunking a banjo with as much skill, if not more, than the men who played with him.

Harlen Damron, Rissie thought to herself as her heart jumped in her chest, *I didn't know that boy could play so good, but I guess he can do anything.*

"Look what his daddy bought my boy for his birthday," Malissa said as Rissie struggled up the big front steps of her porch. "Can't he play that thing?"

Harlen was the son of Malissa's niece and often came with his mother to Malissa's house. He was two years younger than Rissie, but Malissa had seen something in the way the children looked at each other that had escaped both the Hopkinses and the Praters. She had seen Harlen and Rissie catch each other's eyes at different times and she knew that Rissie's faint blush bespoke volumes more than the few words the two had exchanged in their short lifetimes. Malissa smiled to herself; she did not harbor the same gloomy expectation of Rissie's future that most everyone else did.

"You hungry, baby?" Malissa asked. "You want you a little piece of stack cake?"

"No, thank you, Aunt Malissy," Rissie replied without looking at her. Her attention was directed elsewhere. "I just thought I'd come over for a while."

"Well, sit down here and let's listen to the boys." Malissa shooed some of her grandchildren off the swing at the end of *the porch and placed Rissie between her and the side of the house, almost hiding her from the rest of the family. She lit her pipe and, with everyone facing the other end of the porch where the ersatz band had launched into a rousing version of "Soldier's Joy," deftly passed it to Rissie. The charade lasted only a puff or two, however, as more refugees from Harmon's table walked across the creek to listen to the impromptu concert. Slightly disappointed that they could not continue, Rissie was compensated as the families had come together and she blushed again when Harlen finished the tune and smiled at her.*

It had been a good Easter Sunday for the Hopkinses and Praters of Greasy Creek.

It had been a good Easter all across the coal fields of Kentucky, both Eastern and Western. Coal mines were opening daily, jobs were easy to find, and money was beginning to flow into the pockets of mountaineers and flatlanders. Coal was selling at a premium everywhere as steel mills struggled to meet demand for their product.

Just outside Drakesboro in Muhlenberg County in Western Kentucky, a middle-aged couple and an old man sat at their cleared dinner table drinking coffee and talking about the future. There were children playing outside the house, and the old man's eyes were drooping as he, bereft of the physical reserves the whooping mob displayed, gradually succumbed to the Easter dinner just consumed.

"I just wish Acey could have come in for Easter," Mary Jane Willoughby sighed to Grafton, her husband. "I wish he could have stayed here; there's plenty of work for him."

"But Mother, he's making more money than he could have here," her husband gently argued. "You know what he says in his letters: they're desperate for men to work."

"I know, Daddy, but Floyd County's so far away, and now you're going to go, too. How long do you think it will be before we can come?"

"'Bout a year, I suspect," Grafton said. "Mr. Sanders said they need carpenters even more than miners, since they don't have no place for the miners to live and they can't bring anymore in until they get the houses done. He says up in Pike County they're living in tents. He seems like an honest man."

He turned to his father-in-law for support. "What do you think, Dad? You been to Eastern Kentucky, haven't you?"

The old man carefully placed his cup back on its saucer before he answered. His brow knitted as he searched his memory. "Yes, sir, I was," he said, with the military courtesy he had learned a half-century before. "It was a long time ago."

"You think you'd like to go back for a while? We'd sure like to have you with us when we move."

"I reckon I could, if I wouldn't be a burden."

"Dad, you'll never be a burden to us," Mary Jane interjected. Her father had never been the same since her brother James died five years before on the *Titanic*. The old man had staked him in the cattle business with practically all the money he had. It would have been a good business, raising Spanish cattle in New Mexico, but no one expected him to die so young in the way he did. The old man had broken when he heard the news. His son had no grave and he had no fortune to leave the rest of his family.

"No, sir, Paw. We're proud to have you with us," Grafton added, and then began wheezing. Pollen from Mary Jane's spring flowers permeated the house and Grafton's asthma was acting up.

"See Daddy, that's what I'm worried about," Mary Jane cautioned. "You have to promise me you won't go into the mines with all that dust."

"I promise," he said, trying to suppress the tightening of his chest and the overpowering urge to expel what was gathering in his lungs. "I'll be fine, just fine." He took a sip of coffee, placed a reassuring hand on the old man's shoulder and went *outside. He did not want to cause his wife any additional worry. It had been a good Easter.*

On both sides of the Commonwealth of Kentucky, the day was winding down as birds chirped their final pleas for mates to face the year ahead. It had been bright and cheerful; the air already summer-like.

North of Kentucky, a meeting had been hurriedly called in the offices of the McKinney Steel Company in Cleveland and staffers were sitting nervously at a large conference table. Notebooks and fountain pens were at the ready, and everyone knew Price McKinney would soon rush in to issue a flurry of orders. They were not long in waiting.

When McKinney entered the room, the men rose immediately. He placed a valise on the edge of the table, ignoring the chair placed at the head for him and began speaking before his assistant had closed the door behind him.

"Gentlemen, sit down. Thank you all for coming. I have been called to Washington and must leave tonight. As you know, there will soon be drastic changes in the national economy and I expect our expansion plans for the Kentucky coal operations to be severely curtailed. I want all material suppliers to be advised that these contracts must be honored before the national priorities intervene. I want the emphasis on Greasy Creek to be shifted to housing immediately. All supplementary structures not already begun will be placed in abeyance. We will need living quarters for laborers as soon as possible."

The men scribbled furiously as he continued.

"Our tent city will simply have to expand until adequate housing is obtained."

Few of McKinney's staff looked up from their tablets. Some had already refilled their pens from the ink bottles strategically placed on the mahogany table.

"Telegraph Mr. Sanders and ask him to return to the Illinois Basin. He was successful there and we will need

experienced miners. He may offer them more than he did previously to come to Eastern Kentucky." Then he added with a sly smile: "But not too much more, of course."

McKinney grasped the valise he had never opened and issued a final order: "I should be back by Friday. I want progress reports on my desk that morning. We'll meet again Friday afternoon. Good day, gentlemen." The men rose again, but McKinney was gone before half of them could fully stand. They immediately turned to their tasks.

By Friday, their reports would be due and the men knew their boss would scrutinize every word. By Friday, Price McKinney would return after privately meeting with President Woodrow Wilson. By Friday, the families of Pikeville, Greasy Creek and Drakesboro, Kentucky would know full well the urgency McKinney imparted to his staff.

By Friday, the country would have been at war for a full week.

Hunter's Moon

My grandfather Frank was not a hunter, at least not the typical hunter of Greasy Creek, whose men still keep small arsenals of shotguns and rifles. The only weapon I ever knew him to have was an ancient Mossberg single shot .22, and he gave that to me when I was twelve. Neither did I ever know of him killing an animal, except for food. He liked to ramble alone through the hills, when he was still able to climb the mountain trails, but he took no game in those forays. I suspect he simply found comfort in the solitude. It was not that he disliked company; he enjoyed the visitors who came to his house every Sunday, but when they came, they had the burden of conversation.

It was rare to see him smile; his was not a stern face or a dour one and it was strong, but I could sense pain behind it. It was neither a physical pain nor even an emotional pain. It was the worse kind, a pain of the soul. There was always a certain amount of wariness in his eyes, as if he had taken a hard blow and was preparing for another. His face was different from my father's, although I could easily see one in the other. My father smiled constantly and would sometimes elicit a grin from my grandfather and often tried to, but I never really saw Frank Hopkins laugh. My father's attempts at raising my grandfather's spirits were a legacy of his being raised by Rissie, who was the happiest person I ever knew. There was always a twinkle in her eyes, behind the sharp harlequin glasses she favored, and she was the first to laugh at a joke or a funny story, even if it were about herself, although she would often raise her hand to her lips to prevent any of her Old Regular Baptist brethren from interpreting her joy as immodest.

It would be difficult to remember Rissie without a smile, and when she spoke of the past, she did so proudly, as if she were answering a call, as indeed she was, but Frank was reticent. I suspect he talked little about the past because he was afraid if he spoke of any part of it, it would have been a disservice to the rest. It was as if he wanted to keep his memories inside him, protected where they would remain inviolate and sacred. I have no doubt that the past was his vision of heaven and he was more than a little impatient to return to it.

For years I thought Rissie could never have suffered anything like whatever it was that debilitated my grandfather. She told me so many stories of the family I could not keep them all. They tumbled from her as though poured from an overfilled box of toys, and I was careless in tending to them because there were so many. When I would ask my grandfather about the past, he would answer, but not expand on it. It seemed as if he knew that one memory would link to another and then another and he would stop before he would allow himself to reach a point of no return.

"What was it like in France, Papaw?" I once asked him when I was studying World War I in school.

He shook his head as if he would not answer, but then he spoke: "Them old Frenchmans would go out to the fields every day, carryin' their baskets of wine and bread and cheese. They'd walk right by us and pay us no mind at all."

That was all he said that day and in future conversations I retrieved little more information. I had read about the carnage of the Great War; I learned that millions died in repeated futile charges against solid walls of machine-gun fire, young men, the best of their generation, cut down in murderous rows, stumbling over dismembered parts of their predecessors before joining them, brutally partitioned, in the fetid earth. I read of gas shells popping off behind and in front of the trenches, so that the wind would reach the soldiers regardless of which way it blew and the terror of waiting for the wretched fog to pass as the poison crept in around the masks that could never quite seal it all out. Although the war was mercifully brief for the United States, in the Argonne Forest a thousand American boys died each day until the battle was over.

I had seen pictures of white crosses in ordered rows in the American cemeteries, and I knew he would have seen much death, but when I asked my grandfather, he would speak little of those things. He found it most remarkable that French farmers could tend their crops and eat their lunches in one field while a harvest of death littered the others like uncollected wheat.

For a long time, I assumed he had been somehow maimed by the war, although he came back with all his limbs. I thought the holocaust that destroyed most of the institutions of Europe had broken him with the sheer excess of the destruction he surely had seen. But when I saw him on the Old Prater, absorbed in cleaning and precisely decorating certain graves, I knew the pain that crippled him was personal.

Unlike the war of my grandfather, the Second World War, my father's war, took a horrific toll on the boys of Greasy Creek. Rissie told me about the nights they would listen to battery-powered radios for news and wait every day for the mail to arrive at the Greasy Creek post office to see whose homes a letter from the War Department would shatter. It became a daily ritual of dread and heartbreak. For four years, as it was in the Civil War, the specter of loss haunted them. But the First World War lasted barely a year for most American soldiers, and few of Pike County's sons fell then.

On the doughboy statue in Pikeville, raised to commemorate the forty-three Pike Countians who died in the Great War, there are also plaques for World War Two, Korea, and Vietnam. Twenty-six of our boys died in Korea, twenty-four in Vietnam, and two hundred eighteen names crowd the plaque for World War II. In that war, even more Pike County men have their names on largely forgotten plaques in other states, where the sons of our creeks and hollows had moved over the years to escape the cycles of poverty in the coal fields.

But World War I was different. The memory of the Civil War, through its remaining veterans and their stories, was still very much alive when word came to the hills that the *Lusitania* went down in 1915. Not everyone could read, but those who did would relay the newspaper stories to those who could not, and the people of Greasy Creek knew war was coming. When it came, it was essentially the first war to provide them with a common foe. The Spanish-American War had come and gone with little participation and there were brush fires in China and Nicaragua, but the last time so many Greasy Creek boys fought, they fought each other.

On June 5, 1917, those boys were part of a great line coiling through the city of Pikeville, along with all the rest of Pike County's eligible men, waiting to be examined on their fitness for military service. The physical examinations began before daylight and continued until long after dark. Ten million other American boys born between 1886 and 1896 were in similar lines in their own hometowns. Four days before, President Woodrow Wilson announced that anyone failing to sign up for the draft would be arrested and would spend a year in jail for the crime. The boys of Greasy Creek needed no such threat. They had grown up among Civil War veterans, who were themselves not that far removed from the generation of Revolutionary War soldiers who settled Pike County and they were patriotic. Love of country was a core belief, even if most of the boys of Greasy Creek had seen little of it, but they would rather not go if it could be avoided. It had nothing to do with cowardice or fear of death. The possibility of violent death was always a reality in the mountains and the boys accepted the risk. But there were now a host of economic reasons to stay home.

A new mine had opened on Greasy Creek and a huge expansion was planned: an entire town was to be built there and construction had already begun. The flow of supplies up the railroad that was rebuilt on the narrow tracks that once carried thousands of logs out of Greasy Creek to the river had stopped with the war declaration, but until then the river of materiel had been incessant, day and night. The company announced that it would hire every man on Greasy Creek who wanted work, but there were not enough. Men and their families from all over the country would soon be coming and there had to be a place for them to live. Almost overnight, there were more jobs than the mountaineers thought possible. The boys worried less about the war in Europe than whether there would still be work waiting for them in Pike County when they returned, presuming they did.

The first news that filtered into Greasy Creek was that all men had to register and take their physicals, but most of the married men with dependents would be deferred. Suddenly, widows or divorced women with children acquired an allure they could not have imagined a few weeks before. Some of the men brought marriage licenses to their examinations with the ink still fresh on their signatures. After their physicals were concluded, the men went home, awaiting notice from their draft boards that they would sit out this war or report for service. Nearly all of them found work in the mines while they were waiting, although some of them were buried twice before their orders arrived, first under roof falls inside the mines and finally in their family cemeteries. More than once, soldiers came to Greasy Creek looking for men whose orders went unanswered, and returned to their posts empty-handed.

Frank did not know he would not have to go until the following March, but he and all the boys of Greasy Creek slept uneasily every night after that warm day in June. Orders often arrived late, and little time was given to report to the intake station. Some men were AWOL before they were sworn in. By fall, a few of them had tired of the waiting and joined up, but most of them went about their lives waiting daily for the clerk at the post office to hand over an official envelope from the US government. A few of them consulted the Civil War veterans still alive, to ask them about what they would find when they donned a soldier's uniform, and some sought guidance from nearly-forgotten ghosts wearing faded blue or gray. Because of the threat, more than a few romances blossomed, their urgencies fed by it. Wills were drawn up and signed and the boys began to put their affairs in order.

In spite of all the preparations, on a frosty night in the first week of November 1917, Rissie Hopkins was not worried that any of her brothers would have to leave their homes and their sweethearts to face the Germans and die in battle, not if she had anything to do with it. Her firmness in this belief imputed no supernatural power to herself nor any immortality to any of them, however.

She merely thought that she would kill them first.

"Mommy, tell Rissie she can't go," Frank demanded of his mother as he stood anxiously at her kitchen door. Lila was at the stove, stirring a pot of beans and did not want to get involved in the fracas. "It's cold and she could get hurt." Harrison had escaped to another part of the house and left the decision to his wife. Because of his cleft palate, it was difficult for him to speak normally at any time, but when he was stressed his words were nearly unintelligible. Lila usually spoke for her husband in family matters, to save him from embarrassment, but she was as speechless as he would have been. She did not want to take sides among her children.

Frank would not look at his sister, who stood defiant in front of the brother she loved the most, but whose head she now wanted to rip from his shoulders. Neither would he mention the obvious, that her wobbly gait, caused by the clubfoot she was born with, made the steep, uphill journey to Ripley Knob in the darkness dangerous at best. He loved Rissie and was protective of her, but her demand surprised him.

The Hopkins brothers and their friends were going on a hunt, perhaps the last any of them would attend, since orders could arrive any day. The boys had looked forward to this, the best hunting night of the year. The moon rose early and the skies were clear. It was time for a hunt, the crops in, the potato holes filled with Irish potatoes, sweet potatoes, and cabbage heads, and covered with straw and earth to protect them from the frost. Hogs had been killed and scraped, and smokehouses puffed daily with curing meat. Bunches of onions were tied together and hung on the porch joists to dry for winter. Strings of shuck beans streamed down from the walls, coal houses were filled and cords of wood chopped for the coming cold weather. All the chores were done and the boys could now reap some reward for their summer labors. The boys deserved a little fun.

The trip to Ripley Knob to listen to the hounds was a ritual on Greasy Creek, and because of the occasion, the boys did not want a girl, any girl, to go with them. Frank was unpleasantly surprised that this would be an issue. Rissie, who had accompanied her brothers to Greasy Creek's highest peak many times before, was incensed that she would not be allowed to go this time. But although she would not admit it, she knew their argument was valid.

The hills were not fully recovered from the clear-cutting of decades before, and the demands of the company had taken most of what was left. Most hillsides were now covered only with saplings, upright and thin like fishing poles, unworthy descendants of legends barely remembered, and scarcely taller than reeds on the riverbank. In the meadows, exhausted briars of the summer's huge crop of blackberries would have posed a formidable barrier to young men with strong limbs and feet, let alone a crippled girl of thirteen. Compounding the defensive cloak the hills had created, there were yet the rotten, tangled branches of the lost great trees: the weathered detritus of another age, where rattlers and copperheads would hide until spring.

But none of this mattered to Rissie.

"I can so go," she answered. "I been there as many times as he has, day or night. He might have to leave tomorrow and he just don't want me with him." Her upper lip quivered almost imperceptibly, the pink scar from her nostril to her mouth reddening above her pursed lips. The other boys waited outside in the darkness to avoid becoming casualties of the battle now joined in Lila's kitchen. They knew the value of discretion in any fight with tiny Rissie Hopkins.

"They're just goin' to go up there and smoke," Rissie said accusatively. "That's all they're goin' to do, just smoke." Rissie conveniently disregarded the fact that Mammy allowed her to puff from the corncob pipe she smoked until she died.

When he chanced to look, Frank could see the fire of Mammy's black eyes reignited in Rissie's pale blue irises. He could not help but smile at the unfairness of her argument and noted with no small pride that Rissie was Mammy embodied, as if it were the eyes of the Hopkins legend-keeper herself that blazed in front of him. He knew that of all Mammy's grandchildren, it was Rissie whom the old woman had passed on the combative spirit that made the clan what it was.

He also knew that Rissie would not accept that her brothers' potential last night on Greasy Creek would be spent without her, and he snorted with frustration. In the morning, the boys of Greasy Creek might receive their orders and would have to make their way immediately to Pikeville to climb onto the train that would take them far away from home. They would join the thousands of young men pouring out of the Kentucky hills and across the country to prepare for the fight with the Kaiser.

The Hopkins brothers and other boys were waiting in the moonlight outside Harrison's big house, their hounds baying impatiently for the hunt to begin. There was Bud, Rissie's oldest brother, who had deftly avoided the clash embroiling Frank and

Rissie. There was Willie, her second youngest brother, who was proud to share a name with Will, who was sometimes called Big Will to distinguish him from the younger boy. Will was the oldest of the last three sons of Elisha Hopkins and had been raised by Harrison after the legend died thirteen years before. All Harrison's children considered them their brothers. And even Jessie, her youngest brother at nine years old and a twin to his sister Bessie, was there. Other boys, children of neighboring families or new heads of households who had left the beds of their young wives, also joined the group.

Hooker Hopkins, the youngest of Elisha's last brood, was married, had a child, and had already received his deferment. He would not face the Huns, but wanted to be with his brothers this night. Paris, who was the middle child, was also married and had four stepchildren. He had his deferment as well, but like Hooker, he wanted to go on the hunt with the only real family he ever knew. None of them, however, wanted to risk the hurricane facing Frank inside Harrison's house. When Big Will walked through the darkness, all the boys breathed a sigh of relief. They feared the Germans far less than they feared Rissie.

"Women," Paris said, shaking his head. "They'll drive you crazy."

"Well, you must be pretty God damn insane," one of the boys said. "As many women as you got."

"It's just my charm, son," Paris replied with a leer. "The girls like me."

"What's the matter here?" Will asked, sensing the tension among the boys on the great porch that surrounded Harrison's house.

"Rissie wants to go along," said Bud. "She wants to follow all us boys up on Ripley. Frank's in there fightin' it out with her."

"I better go in and talk to her," Will said with a sigh. "She's too much for Frankie to handle on his own." Will had not taken a physical, as he was born in 1885 and was too old to be called in this round of the draft, but he was still the leader of the hunt. He was the older brother to all the Hopkins boys as well as most of the young men of Greasy Creek. Tall and courtly, Will was even more the older brother to Rissie, who saw him as the physical representation of the legends Mammy had told her of Elisha, of his brother Joseph, the Confederate soldier who never came home, of the Old Ones, whose stories, to her frustration, seemed to be more and more unimportant in the strange, manic bustle that now permeated life throughout Pike County.

With the new mine already opened on Greasy Creek and a new town under construction, in addition to all the new mines and towns in Pike County, an unfamiliar prosperity seemed to be lurching drunkenly through the hills. Only Rissie seemed to have misgivings; most of her brothers and the other boys of the creek seemed less worried about the war they would soon be fed into than the jobs they could lose if winning it took too long.

Will understood Rissie's unease. He had just been brought back from Wolfpit and made foreman in the new Greasy Creek mine. Since coal production was a priority, Will did not expect to go to war, but he too wanted to spend as much time as he could with the boys who might not come back. He knew what war could mean. He remembered well his father's last night on earth, in the cabin on Ripley Knob high above Greasy Creek, when the old man called fruitlessly to the ghosts of forty years before to stay with him, to not take sides in the great conflict that eventually consumed them all.

That fabled cabin was the rendezvous for the night's hunt, as the boys could light a fire in the crumbling fireplace and reminisce while the dogs did the work. It was a favorite spot for the Hopkins family, all of them, including Rissie, who never complained when she made the hard trek up the hillside to that place. Will knew that was why Rissie wanted to go with her brothers. She wanted to remind them of the legacy of their family before they marched into battle, she wanted them to remember the glory of the Boys of Greasy Creek.

With her crooked teeth because of the cleft palate, an afflic-
tion she shared with her father, although hers had been repaired
as well as it could have been for those days, and with the awk-
ward gait caused by her clubfoot, Rissie knew she would never
find a man. Neither did any of the family presume that she
would marry. But her infirmities made her strong and she had
accepted her fate. She often wished she had the comely smile or
the graceful feet of the other girls of the creek, but she knew she
could not have competed with them anyway. Her role in the
family was to take care of her parents as they grew old and to
keep the stories of the family alive. It was a burden she took on
happily; she regretted only that Mammy had not lived longer to
tell her more of the legends she was compelled to repeat.

Will knew Rissie's mind and knew his work was cut out for
him. If she were to be tamed this night he would have to do it.

Lila breathed a sigh of relief when Will opened her kitchen
door and she saw who was, to all intents and purposes, her
oldest boy, although in truth he was her half-brother. Lila was
the youngest daughter of Elisha's last wife Mary and, presuma-
bly, her first husband, and Mary had refused to give up her child
when she left him for Elisha, who was twice Mary's age, in 1878.
When Elisha grew older, and turned more and more from the
present to the past, Mary became frustrated with inattention. It
was an easy step to find other companionship. Lila's actual
father was the result of one of Mary's previous assignations, and
she began searching for new ones, neglecting her husband and
her family in the process. After a time, Mammy had seen enough
of life in Elisha's household and took Lila home with her to raise
along with her own two sons. Mary acquiesced and Mammy
would have taken the boys as well, but Elisha would not let them
go. Lila was not his child, but the boys were his own flesh and
blood.

"You're not takin' my sons!" he told her bluntly, but Mammy
knew they would eventually come on their own to join their
sister.

Harrison fell in love with Lila the first time he saw her, but thought he would never marry because of his harelip and his struggle to speak. Over time, he learned that Lila did not need his voice. She saw what his eyes revealed and she eventually fell in love with him as well. In 1889, over Elisha's protests, Harrison and Lila were married at Mammy's house, where so many of the boys and girls of Greasy Creek had made their vows. It was only one of many marriages held at Mammy's; her home was a sanctuary for the lost and love-lost young people of Greasy Creek as long as she lived.

As the years began to weigh on Elisha, Mary began to spend less and less time at home, and their boys gravitated to Harrison's house or Mammy's. After Elisha died in 1904, Harrison and Lila took the boys and a seriously ill Mary into their home and closed the Ripley Knob cabin for good.

Will would have admitted, even before his parents died, that he loved Harrison and Lila as much as he loved his real parents. The younger boys, Paris and Hooker, had only a limited memory of the strength of their father and the beauty of their mother before she fell into ruin, and easily transferred their love to Harrison and Lila. After Mary passed away, Will became the older brother to all eight of Harrison's children, but in deference to his father, he referred to her as Aunt Lila, although he knew she relied on him as any parent would rely on her oldest child.

Will knew Lila's dilemma: on one hand, she knew her boys wanted only the company of men this night. She knew they needed the strength they could draw from the companionship of other boys who would soon be soldiers, and the release they would have by confiding their fears away from the presence of women. But she also knew that Rissie, in spite of her infirmity, was as determined as a mountain goat and could walk the trail to Ripley Knob with her eyes closed. She visited it regularly, with her family or alone, cleaning the lonely graves and planting crepe-paper flowers every year on Decoration Day.

Lila knew the love her daughter had for her brothers and for the boys who would soon face a perilous journey, possibly the last one of their lives. Mammy had taught her well, she thought, had taught her that those most in need of protection frequently decline it and it was her duty to protect them anyway. She would not intervene in anything that would dispute Rissie's charge, and when Will opened the door, she felt she could breathe again.

"Sissy, can I talk to you a minute?" Will asked as he closed the door softly behind him. Rissie looked at him and slumped. She knew Will's purpose when he entered and she knew she would not be allowed to go on the hunt.

"I just want to go with my brothers," Rissie said, her defenses crumbling with Will's kindly smile.

"I know you do," he replied. "But won't you let me take the boys with me this time and then when they come home, we'll all go up on Ripley and they can tell you some stories for a change." Rissie's ruined upper lip began to tremble as he spoke, and he knew she would agree as he had used the strongest weapon in his arsenal.

"I just wanted to go with my brothers," she nearly whispered, her voice cracking in defeat. Will knew she had capitulated and put his arms around her as Frank slipped out the door. "Be careful around Lige's grave," she sobbed to her brother. "And Aunt Mary's. And Mamaw Phoebe's and Aunt Sally's." She remembered no one of whom she spoke, but she remembered the responsibility Mammy gave her.

Will was still ministering to Rissie as Frank rejoined the group outside.

"Can we go now?" Bud asked as he finished rolling a cigarette and licking the paper. Frank's Pyrrhic victory over his sister had subdued his celebration.

"I guess," Frank replied, picking up his lantern, which was the only weapon he carried. Few others were armed, no rifles at all would be found among the boys, even though it was a hunt. They would have been only additional entanglement in the brush. Some of the boys carried pistols they had purloined from their fathers, along with a few bullets they had managed to collect, but no one had any real interest in killing their prey. If the dogs managed to dispatch a fox, then that was merely the natural order of things. And although they would gladly have shot a raccoon or a fox that invaded their chicken coops, they did not want to eliminate the few sporting animals that still roamed the hills. They loved to seek them out on moonlit nights for the pleasure of listening to the dulcet harmonies of hounds on the chase. Killing was not the purpose of this night's hunt.

Will joined them after Rissie was safely mollified, and the boys turned to the upland path beside the barn and released the dogs as soon as they cleared the pasture behind it. In the stark moonlight, no lanterns were needed and the boys walked in single file across trails tramped by long-forgotten buffalo. By the time they reached the top of the ridge, the hounds had locked onto a scent and the boys would follow the ridgeline to Ripley, where they would camp in the darkness and listen to the serenade.

On the way, they passed what remained of the cabins where Indians lived before they disappeared, along with the great trees, decades before. None of the boys remembered either the Indians or the trees, although there were still massive stumps to confirm that giants once lived on Greasy Creek. They knew the stories, since Rissie had told them repeatedly, but now there was little to prove that a different race had once walked on Greasy Creek. Yet every time the boys walked through the camp, they could feel a presence, like someone was watching them, but they were not apprehensive. It was much the same feeling they had at play, when they knew their parents or grandparents were close by, and they were secure in the knowledge they would be protected. They knew they would not feel that in the future.

As the boys approached their final destination, the top of Ripley Knob shined fiercely in the moonlight. From there, they could see and hear for miles, and the derelict cabin below the peak stood out clearly. Generations of Hopkinses had lived there, the last being the patriarch who built it with his brother when they were children. It seemed that the earth was gradually reclaiming the structure, as it had already reclaimed the Indian homes. Moonlight shone through the holes in the roof and much of the window glass had been broken. In a few years, the cabin would burn to the ground during one of the forest fires that raged through the tinderbox piles of decades-old limbs of the great trees. But for now, it was a favorite place for all of the hunters of Greasy Creek to sit and smoke and be entertained by the songs of the hounds and, perhaps, commune with the spirits of all those who had sat there before.

"Boys, I think I can see the dogs," one of the youthful hunters said as the group settled in. "God damn it, I think they're goin' down Hopkins Creek. Shit!" A digression into the creek named for Elisha and Joseph was to be avoided, for the fox could head for the river and swim across at the ford, breaking the trail the hounds were vainly and wildly following. Their baying became faint and eventually stopped altogether.

Bud finished building a fire in the dilapidated fireplace and leaned back against it to roll another cigarette. Will took the other side of the hearth and looked around the ruin, now revealing itself in the rising glow. Only Will had a clear memory of the house when the house was alive. He stared at what was once the bedroom wall, laced with moonbeams dissolving in the firelight, and remembered again the night his father died thirteen years before.

"Maybe we should have brought Rissie along," Bud grumbled. "Those dogs are gone."

Will was reminded that Rissie was born the same year Elisha died and he remembered Mammy's death, eight years later, and how Mammy had taken to Rissie as soon as she was born. It was not just sympathy for the child and her infirmities. Mammy had seen something in Rissie. Mammy had a gift and she knew that Rissie shared it. She also knew that her time on earth was drawing to a close and anointed Rissie the storyteller of the family before she could even speak. That's the way Mammy wanted it, he thought. He remembered how weak Mammy became before she died and when she told a story, Rissie would sometimes have to complete it as her grandmother's voice gave out. Mammy would nod in quiet satisfaction as the young girl spoke.

Mammy trained her well, Will thought. Maybe we should have brought Rissie along after all.

As the baying became more distant, the boys surmised that their hunt would be short-lived, unless the dogs crossed another scent. In a few minutes, only the wind through the few great trees that had survived the holocaust of the 1880's could be heard. The young trees barely whistled in the breeze. In the silence, the boys became reflective.

"You reckon all that stuff actually happened?" one of them asked. "I mean, all that stuff about the Civil War Rissie talks about?" Few of the soldiers from the great conflict were still around and they did not hold much interest for the young people of Greasy Creek, who were too caught up in the moment, in the new opportunities for prosperity. Now, with another war looming, the thought of brothers fighting brothers seemed even more remote; not when Huns were clearly the enemy and the fight going on a world away in places whose names they could not even pronounce.

"Oh, it happened," Will said. "Pappy told me it did, but I can't tell the stories like she does.

"That old stuff don't matter no more," one of the boys interjected. "But I do like to hear Rissie talk. She does right good for a girl." On that the group could agree. Rissie's stories were magnetic, and what was unsaid was that her stories would give some function to her life, since she was hare-lipped and crippled and would never have a family of her own. But then some of the boys wondered if they themselves would ever marry, or if they would have the chance. The question of their own mortality was beginning to overshadow their joy.

"Well, Frankie, are you gonna marry Miss Manie or not?" another one of the group demanded. Manie Ethel Coleman, who lived on the right fork of Greasy Creek, was a beauty. She had skin the color of fresh cream and a smile that easily disarmed the most aggressive suitor. More than a few of the boys had gone to sleep at night remembering the way her deep chestnut hair, glowing with auburn streaks, flowed like a mountain stream across her shoulders, but they had all learned that the only suitor she wanted was Frank.

"It wouldn't be fair," Frank said. "Marryin' somebody just to stay out of the war. What if you get called up and get killed? What if you have children? Who'd take care of 'em if you was dead?" Frank was speaking truthfully. He had yearned for Ethel from the first time he saw her on the playground of the Middle Greasy School, but he knew he would be going to a place where other boys, probably with sweethearts of their own, would try their best to kill him and he did not want the distraction of worry, no matter how much he loved her.

"You think we'll all make it back?" one of the boys asked. In the moonlight, the peak of Ripley Knob glowed brightly. "I mean, they say they've already killed millions and millions over there."

"What do you think about it, Frankie?" he inquired seriously. "I guess I'm a little bit scared, I guess."

Frank struggled for a reply.

Only now was the sheer reality of troop trains and final departures beginning to sink in. When orders came, the boys would ride out to the first of many places they had never been before. None of them knew what awaited them, but no one would have shirked his duty because he was frightened. For a boy on Greasy Creek, it was not in his constitution to allow anyone to call him a coward. None would have let live a man who called him such and he would have died to avenge his honor.

Frank knew violent death was not a stranger to the hills. The legacy of the Civil War had not long played out on Greasy

Creek, and its memory had yet to completely dissipate. The earlier comment that the Civil War did not matter was not really true and he knew it, but that war had no relationship to this one. Just as Frank began to form a reply, the hounds, whose voices had been reduced to whimpers as the fox eluded them, announced the discovery of a new objective, and Frank was thankful for the respite. He did not know what to say anyway. This was the first war any of these boys had known, and the thought occurred to all of them that only Rissie, the tiny, younger sister of the Hopkins boys and, it seemed, all the boys of Greasy Creek, would know what the word actually meant.

"They're on the other side of the ridge!" one of the boys yelled as the dogs rushed back toward them. "Let's go 'round there and listen." The group collectively groaned, but gathered up their items, including the lanterns they did not need in the moonlight and trudged a second time through the cemetery. The fire in the crumbling fireplace died down and the worries that were beginning to emerge in the conversation of the boys were temporarily assuaged.

After they left, the wind picked up and the cabin was deserted again as the last embers in the fireplace went out. If a latecomer stumbled through the dark brush to find his brothers and chums, he would have found nothing, although as he approached the cemetery, he might have thought he heard voices coming from the old cabin.

If he sought his friends and went inside, he would have found no one, and he would have shrugged and picked his way through the gravestones to rejoin the gang. In the darkness and the wind, he might have again heard what he thought he had mistaken for voices; he might have even thought he heard a conversation, but he would have known there was no one there.

"Most of them will come home," were the words the straggler might have thought he heard, by a voice he vaguely remembered from childhood. "Practically all of them, this time."

"It ain't the same," another voice, one the straggler would not have recognized could have replied. "Ain't nothing could be the same."

"It's still war," yet a third voice, also long silenced and equally unknown to the straggler, might have joined in. "Boys still die."

But if he paused to listen, the voices would have ceased, and he would have shaken his head, thinking he was mistaken and walked on. The dilapidated cabin he left and the tiny cemetery he walked through would have slipped back into silence, except for the rustling of dry leaves and the baying of the hounds and the faint laughter of the boys on the other side of Ripley Knob.

And Old Ripley itself, that ancient point that heads up the creek named for two brothers now nearly forgotten, towering over the forks of Greasy Creek where the brothers' glory had long faded, stripped of the trees that grew there for millennia, and cold and bright under the Hunter's Moon, stood mute and defiant as it had for ages, watching her sons in their revel, and admitted nothing of the future.

Rumors of War

In early 1918, Price McKinney horrified his fellow steel magnates with a statement he made to the famous statesman Bernard Baruch, "We are all making more money out of this war than the average human being ought to." The United States had entered World War I less than a year before and relatively few American troops were in France, since the bulk of America's new army was winding its way through the great training camps built all over the country. However, American steel companies had been working overtime for years to meet the orders for munitions sold to the British and French militaries, and profits were enormous.

Steelmaking in the United States had always been a cutthroat business, with prices for pig iron and rolled steel fluctuating wildly, but the demand from Europe made the companies extremely profitable. Money was flowing everywhere. Workers in the iron ore fields, the coal mines, the coke ovens, and the mills and factories were ecstatic with their good pay, and executive pay was astronomical. Four officers of Bethlehem Steel voted themselves a bonus and split over two million dollars. Stockholders merely smiled at the company's largesse. Dividend checks were huge, and supplemental dividends were paid, it seemed, as soon as the regular checks cleared the banks.

With unfilled domestic orders for ships and guns and foreign orders begging, the steel industry was beside itself with glee. It had never made so much money. It was not unusual to see steelmakers' common stock rise a thousand percent in a year. In spite of its war debt, the country's gross national product boomed. American capitalists secretly hoped for a long war to continue the flow of wealth. The ballrooms of their mansions glowed in unsuppressed splendor as lavish parties swirled until daylight and Strauss waltzes filled the air as the countries where the music originated and the aristocracy that fostered it crumbled into history.

But even the capitalists knew their excess would have a short life. Germany took note of the performance of the first American troops and shuddered as swarms of doughboys disembarked at La Havre. Spies in America sent back word of the impregnable war machine producing men and materiel, and when the last German offensive spent itself, peace feelers began to emanate from Berlin.

That was why the other captains of industry were so upset with McKinney. The war would not last and they felt betrayed that he would make such a statement, although it was true. McKinney knew they had little to worry about if they would only think ahead. Their profiteering would not end that abruptly. After the war ended, orders would pour in to rebuild the shattered infrastructure of Europe and the steelmaking business would continue to boom, along with the coal mines of Eastern Kentucky, where young men had created a serious labor shortage when they were called for the draft.

As world wars go, World War I was minimally expensive for the United States, in both financial and human cost. Huge sums were appropriated for the war, but most of the money was never used. No sacrifice among Americans could match the destitution and toll in lives the war inflicted on Europe and, in fact, most American troops did not die in battle, in spite of the thousand-men-a-day toll of the Argonne. Instead, the greatest number of casualties came from disease, much like the Civil War, and the largest culprit was the flu. Spanish Influenza, unfairly named because it was first reported in the Spanish press, was the single worst killer and did not choose one side over the other. It was merciful in one way, that it hastened the end of the Great War. If the warring armies had not been decimated by the plague stalking their ranks, war would have undoubtedly droned on longer and Americans would have been drawn into wasteful trench warfare, the very thing the American commander, John Joseph Pershing, wanted to avoid.

In America, patriotism flourished throughout the short war, while Europe, with its economies shattered and famine stalking its people, was beginning to topple its empires from within. Bread and conscription riots lurched from country to country, and Russia's three-hundred-year-old Romanov Empire disappeared. But for the United States, this war was the first one for the entire country to unite behind since the Revolution. After the *Lusitania* outrage, America's collective anger essentially removed all the lingering sectional differences.

After the First World War ended, the country would continue to honor its glorious, if tardy, contribution to Allied victory. For years, doughboy statues were erected on courthouse lawns and accompanying patriotic speeches would be heard across the country. Buildings and bridges were named for heroes, and the government paid for voyages to Europe for Gold Star mothers to visit the well-tended graves of their lost sons.

For the boys of Greasy Creek and places like it all across the country, where men obediently reported for the draft or volunteered according to their own concepts of duty and love of country, the war was real, and the experience profound. For my grandfather, whose dog tags I found in the old steamer trunk he left me after his death in 1973, the experience was nearly unfathomable.

That may have been why he could not speak of it. What he told me was never as detailed as the stories his son's generation told at the American Legion hall my father ran for years. Yet he did tell Rissie much of what I can speak of now, and in turn she told me. When I received his service record, I confirmed again more of the truth that she had always spoken.

Unlike the Civil War stories I tended to dismiss as mostly myth, I knew the stories Rissie told me of my living family were true. I could see the crippled old men the strong young men of her stories became. I remember my grandfather's lungs rattling until his death, and my great-uncle Bud Hopkins's final years in a wheelchair, or my great-great-uncle Paris Hopkins's poverty and final years in a soldier's home. I did not know that Paris could have had a deferment because he had four children, but he would not let his friends and brothers go to war without him.

Frank Hopkins' Dog Tag

I could see the old men of my family bent and bowed and I knew that all they wanted, every minute of every hour they were away, was to come home to the hills and marry the girls they left behind them, and restart the lives that had been put on hold while they marched off to make the world safe for democracy.

My grandfather served exactly one year, from March 8, 1918 to March 8, 1919. One year. Exactly one year. But that was enough, and he came home a different man than the boy who had gone away to war. But he also came back to a different Greasy Creek, although the war was far from the only reason for its transition.

*   *   *

Frank thought it more than strange to be back so soon; it was almost like he had no right to be there, or like he was dreaming. In one way it seemed only yesterday that his orders had come to the Alka post office, which was overwhelmed with mail for the new Greasy Creek camp. A new post office for the camp was planned, but the tiny building at the mouth of the hollow named for a patriot of the Revolution groaned with letters and packages. Word had already passed him as he walked across the hill to Gardner Fork, and his family was waiting when he walked into his father's front yard with the envelope in his hand. He remembered Rissie loping across the yard in spite of her clubfoot and clutching him tightly, and his mother, with tears in her eyes, standing immobile on Harrison's big front porch, wringing her hands and mouthing a prayer that he would come home alive.

In a way, it seemed that the orders had not come to him at all, but to someone else, some callow youth who had left Greasy Creek and never returned. Yet he had come home, and when the train hissed to a stop at the Pikeville depot, his heart raced with that realization.

Frank would not wait for the shuttle to Greasy Creek after he disembarked from the train and neither would most of his comrades. There was a noisy, flag-waving crowd at the station, not as big as the crowd that sent him off barely a year before, but he had not expected much of a crowd at all. He had heard there were laws that forbade public gatherings, laws left over from the paranoia of the Spanish Influenza pandemic and the losses of the pandemic itself. Manie Ethel had written him about the horror on Greasy Creek, the bloody deaths that seemed to attack only the healthiest bodies and the dread everyone felt from never knowing whether it would strike them and the fear they would be dead by evening, no matter how good they felt at daybreak.

She wrote him that Harmon had lost one of his daughters and nearly all her family to the Flu, that she was buried with her youngest child in her arms and the other three buried beside their mother, all in a line, all victims. Other family members died just as tragically and just as horribly, and no family on

Greasy Creek was spared. For months, no one felt safe or immune. The new public health department in Pikeville was overwhelmed with completing death certificates, and on the cause of death line most of them read, "Spanish Influenza. No doctor present." The few doctors that practiced in Pike County were equally exhausted from tending to so many cases, since most of their colleagues had been called into service.

In the Pike County town of Elkhorn City, near the Virginia line, the gravedigger at the city cemetery had so many burials that he moved into his tool shed on the cemetery grounds and had his family bring him meals. Even then, the bodies accumulated so rapidly he had to build another shed to cover the caskets until he could consign them to the earth, but few families complained; the law prohibiting public gatherings applied to funerals and during the height of the terror, it was rare for anyone to attend his lonely work. By the time the pandemic had sputtered out, several times as many Pike Countians died as the boys that fell in uniform.

Frank knew intimately of what she spoke. He had seen much the same on the troopship that carried him to France. That ship had seemed a coffin to him, a sealed metal coffin he could not escape, and every night he prayed that he would not be taken in the hideous, indescribable way his shipmates were dying, their lungs filling with blood, their minds lost, as the murderous thing took its daily toll. Every day men died and were given over to the sea in weighted, canvas bags. He had stood guard a half-dozen times as the platforms were upended, sending the olive-drab shrouds with their festering, bloated cargo to the bottom of the Atlantic.

He wondered many times how combat could be worse than what he had seen on the trip across the ocean. He could not fathom the concept of burial at sea, the incredible loneliness such a thought imparted to him, and the insignificance of a human body cast into a limitless ocean with no marker, but after what he had seen in battle and afterward, he might have preferred such a resting place for himself.

It's over, he thought, but he had to keep reminding himself of the fact.

A few of the families from Greasy Creek had come to Pikeville to welcome back their sons, and some of Frank's kin were there, but the one he wanted most to see was still at home. He searched through the crowd to find her, just in case, but was more relieved than disappointed that she was absent. He did not want to take a chance on the Flu's alleged departure. He feared that the beast might still lurk in the crowd, undetected and ready to strike again.

Frank yearned for Manie and for his family. He had never been away from them this long in his life. He kept all their letters and re-read them daily. In all Manie Ethel's letters and all the letters he received from Rissie and his mother, no one mentioned that Manie herself nearly died from the flu and had yet to fully recover. She merely told him she had taken ill, but was all right now. She thought she was lucky, since the flu seemed to seek out the healthiest, those in the absolute prime of their lives, and they would die within hours. She did not tell him the flu had left her weakened and consumptive, as it had most of its survivors in the hills. Only later, would Manie and Frank admit to each other how close they both came to death.

But on this day, celebrations were the order of the day: the boys had come home. There was a brass band playing patriotic music and a fiddle player bowing an old soldier's song. He remembered that fiddlers on Greasy Creek said it was something from the Civil War, although it had been around for hundreds of years, maybe longer. Frank knew now that there had always been soldiers. For Frank Hopkins, however, his soldiering days were over.

"You want to wait for the train, Bud?" he asked his brother.

"Not me, Frankie," Bud replied. "Let's get the hell on home."

Frank noted absently that there were politicians working the crowds in cheerful disregard of the laws they were sworn to uphold. He avoided them as he made his way through the sea of well-wishers. The festivities were makeshift but heartfelt. Telegraph workers had kept the wires alive as the train made its way up the tracks bordering the Big Sandy from Catlettsburg and Frank could easily hear the cheering at every town over the scream of the train whistle, long before the town came into view. He was honored and humbled by the turnout, but he had little interest in amusement; he just wanted to go home.

Like the rest of the boys, Frank had slept little since his discharge at Camp Taylor outside Louisville several days before. The seats and aisles were full as they crowded on and off a half-dozen trains since their hurried separation from the Army. Between times, they would stretch out on the floor of the stations or under the porticos where cargo and baggage was placed, anywhere to merely close their eyes and dream of home, although they would often have to force their eyelids shut because they were too excited for sleep. All of them were like drunken men in half-stupor, trying to conjure sleep to replace the images they had seen in the last year with the images of the place and the people they had left. But there were things they could never forget.

In spite of their exhaustion, when they rounded the last curve and Pikeville appeared, they were suddenly alive with energy to finish the journey. The evening shuttle would not arrive for hours, and with rails clogged with the trains the railroads had sent out to help get the boys home, it could be even longer. Along with Bud and most of the boys that left the creek a year earlier, and at a pace that seemed unlikely, given what he had endured over the last year, Frank began the walk home.

Still wearing their heavy overcoats from their winter in Europe, the boys of Greasy Creek paused only long enough to taste the lemonade and sample the cookies the young girls had baked for them. A few of the boys decided to remain, to take advantage of the dashing figures they presented in their uniforms and the salutary effect they had on the young girls, but most of Frank's party soon turned to the river, where they were too impatient to wait for the ferry and walked through town to cross the bridge in the early spring sunlight. In spite of the heavy duffel bags they carried, stocked with the uniforms the government let them keep along with their mustering-out pay and the contraband souvenirs they brought home, the boys shouldered then easily for their last march. After all, they were soldiers; they were young, and strong.

More importantly, they were alive.

As they straggled up Chloe Creek away from the river, a few boys found their fathers riding toward them with horses. They climbed on and offered rides to their chums, with some accepting, in spite of the danger involved in riding behind a wild boy who had just discovered he was free again. All of them marched, however, in a decidedly non-military fashion. *We may still wear the uniform, they thought, but by God, we ain't soldiers no more.* No more sergeants, no more lazy officers, no more God damn death; they were just Greasy Creek boys again.

For a year they had served and even to impatient young men who measure time in agonizingly slow increments, it seemed to have passed rapidly—basic training, advanced training, embarkation, the ghastly ocean voyages, the sheer terror of plunging into battle. All of it had passed in the space of one year. But in spite of the war's brevity, they could never forget what they saw.

As Frank paced up the railroad track, he would find himself alternately walking in a decidedly civilian lope or marching precisely as if he were still on parade. In his mind, he was still unsure of his status, and the images of what he had left behind fought mightily with the images of what he had left or what he was returning to.

He wondered if that struggle would go on as long as he lived, if the images wrestled not just for his conscious mind, but also for his very soul.

For Frank and the other boys of the 84th Division, it was incomprehensible that after he had trained so hard and endured the withering profanities of sergeants for months, he would spend barely thirty days in battle. For some of the later arrivals of his division, it was even more surprising; they arrived in France just in time to be herded back to embarkation points to go home.

Frank was assigned to Battery F, 326th Field Artillery, and manned a French-made 75mm gun, since American guns were still rolling off the lines of American factories. His hearing had already been damaged in training, and he expected that he could lose all of it when he went into action, but the division itself never fired a shot under its own command. Instead, when the 84th arrived in France, it was immediately "skeletonized" and its units dispatched to other Argonne divisions that had been worn down by the last gasp of the German Army as it tried to break the relentless American advance.

Frank's battery had been sent to fill holes in the line of batteries of another division. Bewildered that he was sent away from his brother and the other boys he had trained with, but he had little time to think. For nearly a month, day and night, he was deafened by the constant blast of his own gun and the guns of surrounding batteries. He had little sleep and witnessed the response of the heavier German guns as they secured their range to zero in on the American lines, and occasionally scored hits, blasting guns, caissons, horses, and bodies of men into the air. But he was lucky, in a fashion. In spite of the constant fear of a direct hit, his battery was almost never touched.

Except for the last days of the war.

After three days of firing, his commander noted a lull in the artillery from the other side. Frank heard him speak to his corporal, and thought he heard him say something about gas.

Frank had trained for poison gas, but his mask dangled unused from his belt and he had never pulled it on in combat.

Had Frank had known anything of the politics of war, he would have known that by 1918 gas was coming back into vogue. It had not been used recently as much as it was during the early days of the Great War, when it was used to create holes in the enemy lines. It was used less because it had the unsettling effect of drifting back over the lines it was supposed to protect. The French used it first, then the British and then the Germans, who perfected the horror and produced more than any combatant, but all of them began to turn away from gas because of its unpredictability.

Then the war neared its end.

As both the opposing forces wearied and word of peace feelers went out, commanders husbanded their troops and ordered their artillery to use everything in their arsenals. *Everything.* Now more gas shells than ever were flung by both sides. The terror had returned with a vengeance.

Frank knew what gas could do to a man. He had seen its casualties when he passed through sick call at the hospital in Neuvic, where his regiment was based, before going to the front. While he waited to be declared healthy enough to die in combat, he could hear the gurgling of men in their death throes in nearby wards, men who had failed to put on their masks in time or pulled them off rather than struggle to breathe through the heavy filters. He hoped that if he had to die, it would be sudden and not as wretchedly as the pour souls he saw writhing toward the end in hospital wards.

"Jesus, Mary and Joseph!" he heard his lieutenant say as gas shells began thudding near his position. When the muffled explosions ensued, he knew what he was facing.

"Gas! Gas!" the lieutenant shouted.

That part of Frank's training came back to him and he knew what to do—pull on the mask! Retreat to the rendezvous point! Run! It was nearly dark, and the men had only perfunctorily been told where to assemble if they had to leave their batteries. In the greening twilight Frank ran as fast as he could. Even he was surprised to find that he had run in the right direction. Half the men, however, did not make the rendezvous, and some of them never arrived, running straight into the vile cloud that engulfed them like the robes of Hell's messengers, invisible demons that grasped and carried the tormented souls of the soldiers immediately into the Pit. Frank saw their twisted bodies, burned, swollen and postulant, as they were carried back behind the lines.

Within hours, the unit reorganized and went back to their guns.

"Wash everything!" he was told. "Touch nothing until it is washed down. Do not sit on the ground. This is Yperite; it can still kill you."

Frank had heard of Yperite, which was another name for mustard gas, although he knew no more of what it meant than the words chlorine and phosgene. He had learned the terms in training, but had not yet experienced them. Yet whatever it was, he knew it was bad and he followed orders scrupulously.

Two days later, German artillery zeroed in on his line and neighboring emplacements began to vanish in the barrage. The air seemed full of earth and cordite and shrapnel and body parts. He knew his battery could suffer the same fate and he turned to his commander just in time to see the young man's head disappear from his body, which crumpled to the ground like a wet quilt falling from a spring clothes line. With no one to direct them, the men dived into a nearby shell crater for sanctuary. As soon as Frank fell into it, his hands and eyes began to burn and his lungs felt like he was breathing fire.

Only once before had Frank felt like he was going to die, and that was when he was still a child and innocent. He was barely sixteen and had chased a displaced swarm of honeybees from their crowded former home and hastily tied a bucket to a long pole to capture the mass and place it in a new hive. His father had taught him how to tend bees, and he had robbed the hives under his father's instructions, but had not yet been given leave to attempt something so hazardous by himself. Harrison was not at home when the young queen had taken her brood in search of new quarters, and Frank was fearful he would lose them. He decided to scoop up the sinister, hanging lump on his own.

He could almost taste the honey he would eventually rob when the bucket with all its cargo fell, covering him with maddened bees. All he could think of was a small pool he had built in the creek to keep minnows for fishing. Through the angry cloud that shrouded him he found the creek and fell into it. In pain and nearly drowning, he would come up for air only to find the bees waiting to attack again, and by the time they had given up tormenting him, he was nearly unconscious and swollen to twice his size.

He remembered little of the remainder of that day or the night that followed. He could see phantoms in his delirium. Sometimes it would be his mother or father or Rissie, wiping his face with cool water and plucking the stingers that protruded from his body like cactus spines.

"He ain't going to make it," he heard a disembodied voice declare. "I don't know how that boy is hangin' on. He's going to bust wide open."

"No, he won't!" he heard Rissie say. "Not my brother."

Rissie, he thought, my crippled little sister? Can you save me, Sissy? Can anyone?

He saw ghosts floating near him— Old Lige, in all his stentorian majesty, shaking his head gravely. Mammy was there too. "Don't worry, boy," she said. "You sleep now. You'll be fine."

Two days later, he awoke with pain wracking every bone, every joint in his body, but he was alive, and Rissie, who had not slept or eaten as long as he was in extremis, could smile her broken smile again.

It was the most beautiful sight he had ever seen.

"Did anybody save my bees?" were the first words he spoke.

This time, however, Rissie was on the other side of the world and he wondered how he would survive without her.

"Bloody Hell! Bloody Hell!" he heard a voice above him. "Get out of there! Get out! Quickly now!"

Nearly blind, he forced himself out of the crater and was immediately splashed with water, cold water, water that had not felt so good since Rissie had bathed him after the bee attack.

"Get your clothes off!" someone demanded and Frank complied. "All of them! Christ! Bloody Christ! Yperite stays in the ground. Do you rubes know nothing?"

The water was not enough; the fire in his eyes, his ears, his nose, and all of his skin was only slightly diminished and there was nothing he could do for his lungs. He could not cough, he could not breathe, and the world swirled around him. When he woke up at the aid station, he was still naked.

In spite of his injury, Frank was soon ordered back to his gun. It was now November, and the artillery duels between the American and German gunners had only increased. Day and night the guns roared, but somehow the smell of cordite seemed to ease the burning of his skin and he pressed on with his work in spite of eyes swollen nearly shut and blisters lining his mouth and tongue. He was blackened by the soot and dirt and blood that rained down on him, but he took little notice: he had become an automaton, loading, firing, loading again, firing again, and again and again and again.

And then it was over.

On the exact and gratuitously poetic eleventh hour of the eleventh day of the eleventh month of 1918, the guns, which had never ceased firing from the time Frank arrived in the line, began to fall silent. His new commander held a gold watch in front of him as the minute hand ticked toward 11:00 a.m. and at exactly the top of the sweep, he ordered "Cease Fire!" In the distance, he could hear the last of the guns as other commanders ignored their watches or their orders or simply wanted to extract a final vengeance for all the years of loss and pain. But the silence eventually crept along the front, as if some prehistoric beast had emerged from its lair and forced all subordinate creatures in its way to cower. Not even birds would chirp. The silence became oppressive as the men remained coiled in their positions, ready to continue their work if the Germans did not follow suit, but nothing happened.

After standing erect and white-faced for nearly half an hour, his commander clicked shut the gold case of his watch and slipped it back into his pocket. Frank could see the man tremble as he turned away from his group and wiped his eyes.

Slowly at first, and then in a massive roar, cheers went up from both sides of the front. In line after line, tears followed soon afterward. The reality of the Armistice began to sink in and men scrambled to build fires to make coffee for the first time since they arrived at the Front. As the sulfurous smells dissipated, the gray countryside of France in early winter began to appear in the distance and spectral figures of other soldiers materialized in the haze. By dark, bottles of wine and whisky were found and drained. At times a song could be heard, first with a single voice and then with others joining in, but it would not last long either. There had been truces before and the men remained wary, but eventually the soldiers allowed themselves to believe the war was actually over.

The war that had claimed so many millions of lives and left millions more blinded and broken was done. The war that leveled cities and towns, left fields poisoned with unexploded ordnance for generations, the war that reduced men to inconsequential pounds of flesh, ground and pressed to lubricate the wheels of war machines, the war that had destroyed most of the empires of Europe, the war that had taken most of the boys of Greasy Creek away from home for the first time since the Civil War, and the war that had taken Frank away from Manie Ethel Coleman, had passed into history. The sheer awesomeness of what he had seen would take him years to sort out.

Frank could not understand any of it; one minute the very earth on which he stood was contested, men were ready to die to acquire it, and it rumbled and groaned as if Hell itself were struggling to escape. The next minute there was no longer a claim. There was only an eerie silence; silence as thick as the gun smoke that blotted out the sun above him and covered his face with soot as black as the coal dust that clung to him after a day in the mines. He saw his fellow soldiers straighten themselves from their hunchback poses and watched in amazement as the farmers went about their duties as if nothing had happened.

All during that time, the French who lived near the line came out daily with their food baskets to plow the fields around them, preparing the soil for spring planting. My grandfather would not have known what 'surrealistic' meant, but he experienced it every day as the American guns dueled with their German counterparts, and through the noise and smoke and violent death, the French farmers would nonchalantly walk by, chatting among themselves as if they were taking an evening constitutional.

Battery F stood its post on the edge of the Argonne for another month, but as fears the Armistice would collapse diminished, it returned to base. The 84th Division was not fully reformed however; men were dispatched again to other units throughout their area to assist in cleaning up what four years of war had done. As winter set in, in spite of the blood he constantly coughed up, Frank was ordered out every day, working to pry rusting and mangled equipment out of the frozen earth and load it on carts and trucks to haul away. Mountains of scrap iron appeared; Frank had never seen so much steel. Occasionally, an unexploded shell submerged in mud would complete its unholy mission and punctuate their labors as the Germans took a final toll, even if unknown to them, on the soldiers of the American Expeditionary Force.

Still, it was preferable to casualty detail, when he had to search through what used to be No Man's Land and dozens of simple fields for the shallow graves of soldiers whose bodies would rarely have dog tags, the aluminum identification disks that gave only the name and serial number, still attached to the corpses. In many cases, there was little of anything attached to the torsos of what used to be men: natural appendages, including heads, were often missing, and he never became accustomed to the work. The few passes into neighboring villages and the leave he acquired to visit Paris and even the wine he drank would never wash away the foul taste in his mouth. In truth, he never acquired a taste for wine, unlike his brother Bud, who largely enjoyed both the drink and the young women who served it. Nor would it wash away the memory of what he had seen or ease the constant reminder of his service in the bloody sputum he could never fully cough away. Only the memory of what he left behind sustained him.

Eventually, the division reformed as their work was done and orders came to embark on another overcrowded troop ship. Frank dreaded the return voyage, but mercifully, only a few men were given over to the sea on the voyage home and none as a direct result of the Flu. The beast was apparently sated.

After his mustering-out at Camp Zachary Taylor outside Louisville, exactly one year after Frank was sworn into the Army in Pikeville, Frank was in a daze. Nothing that happened during the past year seemed real to him, not the training nor the ocean or the fierce final battle of the war, not its aftermath, not even the year of his life he had lost. The only thing that was real to him was home and his family and Manie Ethel.

Now he would see her before the sun set.

After the interminable marches through Camp Taylor, after the sea voyages where he had no space to walk, and after slogging through the mud of France, it seemed to Frank that the trip across Chloe Creek was over in a blink, but his impatience grew the closer he came to home. When he got to the river crossing where Pike County was born in 1821, he almost jumped in the Big Sandy to swim across rather than wait for the decrepit ferry with the boys. On the other side of the river were Greasy Creek, his mother and father, his sisters and brothers, his dogs, his bees, and Manie Ethel.

As they walked the railroad tracks up the creek, he would force himself to pause when one of the boys broke away to run up the steps to his home. Everyone was crying. Jubilation erupted with every arrival. He had a dozen hugs to contend with at each house as he was welcomed like a brother, but tension grew with every step he took. His home was nearly at the head of the creek, and every pace that brought him closer was heavier and more difficult.

Frank could see and hear the difference a year made as he walked up the railroad tracks with his chums. Twice they had to get off the tracks, once to let a filled coal train pass out of Greasy Creek and once to permit a train of empty coal gondolas to rumble back up the tracks. He could hear the whistles and bustle of the camp miles away from it and picked up his pace. With visions of a good job, marriage to the girl he loved, and a family to make his father proud of him, he realized he was probably the happiest he had ever been in his life and the most excited.

And strangely, at the same time, the most weary.

The terror and the horror of the past were now overwhelmed by the present; his eyes misted and his knees were weak with the thought that in a matter of minutes he would be there. It was over and he was home and he swore to himself that nothing would ever take him away from Greasy Creek again.

Frank Hopkins knew nothing of the events that led up to World War I. He had never heard of Zola or Dreyfus or Clemenceau, and perhaps only half-understood conversations about them. He had learned a few words of French, most of which he would not repeat, and some German. He knew what a Luger was, but he knew nothing of Krupp Steel or the Age of Privilege that disappeared along with the aristocrats of Europe or the proletarian struggles that soon followed. He could not have found Sarajevo on a map and he knew nothing about the despised Kaiser, except that he had run out on his country when it was defeated. But he knew that in his own small way he was part of history and he was thankful he no longer had reason to be confused or bewildered.

Rissie & Bessie —
By the summer of 1919, almost all the boys of Greasy Creek had come home from the war and the McKinney Steel Company had a Fourth of July Celebration. The company paid for food and watermelons and offered prizes for the most patriotic dresses made by the girls. Rissie and Bessie outfitted themselves in red, white and blue and won the grand prize, which was the honor of leading the parade through the town to the ball field. Rissie carried the flag and marched upright and gracefully in spite of her club foot.

Soon, Frank would learn not to expect reveille to wake him every day. He would learn not to expect death whistling in from the heavens and would not spring out of his chair when the wind blew the front door shut. He would finally learn how French farmers could carry their bread and cheese and wine past his gun every day to work their fields amid the maelstrom that seemed to envelop the world, and he would then pause and reflect on what he had done and how he had escaped alive. One day, he would go into the hills alone and sit down on one of the great stumps that remained from the lumber holocaust of decades before and take out the dog tag he had been given as a soldier and look at it for a last time before putting it into his trunk for the time he would show it proudly to his sons.

And he would pray that they would never see what he had seen, that they would never go unwitting and alone and unprepared into the awesome world outside Greasy Creek, that they would never leave their sweethearts behind them, that he would never again, not ever again in his lifetime, hear drums and cries and moans or rumors of war.

Old Soldiers

*T*he old man could feel the braking of the train in his gut before momentum pushed the rest of his body forward. The ancient wound was still there, nearly sixty years after he suffered it on that summer morning on the parade ground when his horse reared and fell on him. His was a cavalry regiment, and part of the training was to ride through a gauntlet of gunfire to accustom the horses to the sound, although the exercise was as much to inure the men as the horses to the pandemonium they would soon face. His mount was barely old enough to break, and the din was too much for the animal, but at least it was not injured. Through the flames that erupted across his abdomen, the young trooper could feel his guts press against his skin when they lifted him up.

"No, sir!" he told the doctor who wanted to send him home. "Give me a day or two and I'll be fine." The doctor shook his head, but the boy was persistent, and eventually he prevailed. With the help of the camp cobbler, the doctor fashioned a wide belt to compress the boy's wound, a wound that he knew would never heal, and allowed the young soldier to return to duty. Eventually, the boy learned to accept the unremitting pain and press back the constant need to vomit as he rode.

It was a skill that would serve him well as the War unfolded.

His old wound reminded him of those days, but he was surprised that nothing else did on this trip. It did not seem to be *the same place that he had seen during that bleak January in 1865, when he camped at the war-weary little town called Pikeville. He did not recognize the town when the train stopped there, and it wasn't just the new buildings or the new railroad or the bustle of all the towns that lined the river; it was something else. He was surprised that he recognized nothing. Even the hills did not look the same.*

"We're here, Daddy!" Mary Jane exclaimed as the train steamed and snorted to a halt. "I can see Grafton and the children on the landing." The old man smiled when he saw his grandchildren through the smoky window, but his eyes widened at what he saw behind them. He marveled at the sheer number of half-finished houses and buildings in the tiny valley and had to squint at the reflection of sunlight off the newly sawn wood. He easily counted a half-dozen teams of horses pulling carts of lumber to supply the small army of men that swarmed like ants over the construction site.

With the help of his daughter and his cane, the old man left his seat and shuffled to the rear of the car and tentatively descended the steps. His son-in-law greeted him and took his arm as he stepped off. His grandchildren swarmed around him. He had finally arrived. The trip from Muhlenberg had taken them two uncomfortable days, through Louisville and past Cincinnati, along the Ohio to Catlettsburg, where they boarded another train and followed the Big Sandy to Pike County, the easternmost county in the state. After many stops at the river towns and sidings, they came to the spur on Greasy Creek, where the train would unload and load and reverse its engine to back out to the river.

"Well, Dad," Grafton said after he had assisted his wife down the same steps her father had descended, "welcome to Greasy Creek. I want you to meet my boss."

Grafton turned to a short but strongly built man who had just ordered two young men to the baggage car to help Mary Jane retrieve the trunks she had brought with them.

"Dad, this is Peter Prater." The man smiled broadly and extended his hand.

"Glad to meet you, Mr. Willoughby," Peter said.

"Bracken, William Bracken" Grafton gently corrected him. "He's my father-in-law."

"Oh, that's right. I'm sorry, Mr. Bracken," Peter said, smiling. "I forgot." His broad smile continued. "Grafton told me quite a bit about you. Did you have a good trip?"

"Yes, sir," the old man said. He was not sure how to address his son-in-law's employer, who was younger than Grafton, but exuded the dignified power of command. He wondered if Peter had been a soldier.

"Been to Pike County before?" Peter asked.

"Yes, sir," the old man replied. "A long time ago."

"Was it during the War?" Peter asked.

"Yes, sir," the old man said reticently. "I was here with General Stoneman." He was not sure he should reveal that information, but Peter's smile made him feel at ease.

"So was my granddaddy Zeke," said Peter. "He was with the 39th Kentucky." Loose threads began to realign themselves in the old man's memory; he remembered the regiment, but could remember no faces attached to it.

"I was with the 12th," the old man said, pleased with the information. "I'd like to speak to your granddad sometime."

"Well, he's been gone about ten years now," Peter replied softly. "Most of the old soldiers have passed, but there's a few left, mostly Union." Peter pursed his lips in thought.

"Let's see, there's Uncle Bob Damron, he's one of our preachers. He was in the 39th too." Peter thought for a minute longer. "Not too many Confederates still around, though." Then he added with a grin: "Except for my mother. You'll meet her soon enough; she's done taken up with your family."

The old man smiled at the words; he was glad his family had friends here, Union or Confederate. He would like to meet some of the Confederate boys as well.

"Were you in the Army, Peter?" he asked.

"No, sir," replied Peter, still smiling. "I signed up for the draft, but the war ended before I got called." Peter's eyes twinkled as he spoke: "I guess Kaiser Bill heard I was coming."

The old man smiled back. He liked this man.

In a moment, Mary Jane returned with the boys who pushed a small cart with her baggage.

"That tall one's Andrew, one of my boys," Peter chuckled. "He's the oldest. Has a mind to marry, he does."

"Well, I guess we're all ready," announced Mary Jane.

Peter issued a command to the boys, who turned off the ramp into the muddy street. He would have made a good commander, the old man thought, strong, but kind to his men.

"You'll have to pardon the mud for a while longer, Mr. Bracken," Peter informed him. "After we finish the houses, we'll have sidewalks made of concrete. But 'til then you'll at least have a good roof over your head."

"When your son-in-law first come here, he had to sleep in a tent!" Peter laughed. The old man could tell Peter was proud of his handiwork and now the camp was rising into a real town with solid houses, a church, a school, and a hospital.

"Boss, we can make it from here," Grafton said. "I know you're busy and I'll be back on the job as soon as I get them settled in."

"Nonsense," Peter replied. "I want to talk some more to your father-in-law." The old man thought he might be compensating for getting his name wrong, but was still pleased that this obviously important man would take the time to speak to him.

"Well, Mr. Bracken, does Pike County look the same as it did when you first come here?"

Although they had gone only a few yards from the train, the old man was already slowing down. He took a deep breath before answering.

"No, sir, it don't."

"Well, I wouldn't expect it to. The trees are just coming back. You wouldn't believe how many trees we rafted down the river from here. We barely scraped up enough timber to finish the camp. Had to bring in most of it. The old Yellow Poplar Lumber Company just about cleaned us out twenty years ago."

That was what was wrong, the old man thought, the last time he was here the trees were giants. He thought the hills had shrunk somehow.

The group walked slowly, but the old man was breathing hard when they arrived at one of the houses that was, like most of them, generally complete. It had no paint on the new siding and the smell of sawn lumber and fresh plaster permeated the air as he struggled up the few steps to the porch. Peter's boys had already unloaded their cargo and were awaiting his orders. After inspecting their work, he sent them on their way with the cart.

"Is this all for us?" the old man asked in amazement as he looked around his new home. There was a brand-new rocking chair, also unpainted, awaiting him on the front porch. He noted that the house had both front and back porches.

"Well, half of it anyway," Peter chuckled again. "Each house has eight rooms, four on each side. You all will have two up and two down. Another family'll be living in the other side. After your son-in-law and I finish building the houses, we'll paint them and then we'll finish these streets. It'll be a real town soon. If there's anything you need, just let me know." He shook hands again with the old man and went out the door with Grafton. Mary Jane began unpacking her trunks.

"Can I help you, Sister?" the old man inquired.

"No, Daddy," she said gently. "Why don't you go sit on the porch and look around? Me and the children'll take care of all this. You can take you a nap."

The old man shuffled outside and sat down. The chair was comfortable, and he suspected that Grafton bought it just for him. This must have cost him some money, he thought regret-

fully, and he had little to contribute anymore. He so hated to be a burden to his children, but Mary Jane could not leave him all the way across Kentucky any longer. He knew he did not have much time left on this earth.

The old man was amazed at the activity in the camp. The cacophony of hammers and saws was continuous, as though the camp were a vast staging ground for the battle soon to be joined with the mountain. He thought it not unlike other battles he had prepared for, but those conflicts were not with something that did not breathe. Then it was with other young men much like himself, young men who believed in something different from what he did, but believed just as strongly. *I'd like to meet them,* he thought, *if they are still here, and if they would want to meet me. There are so few now that remember those days, and Grafton's job won't last forever. When the camp is finished, we'll go back to Muhlenberg.* Two decades before, he had reserved a place there to rest beside Sarah, his late wife. He often wished he was already with her, and would not be causing his family so much bother. *Maybe I can make some friends while I'm here,* he thought, *so they won't have to tend to me so much.*

He wanted to meet those boys who rode with him, even if he did not remember them, and he also wanted to meet those who rode against him, to say that he understood, and that now they were comrades as well, that they had all fought the good fight and now it was over and they could all be friends again. He hoped it wasn't too late.

As a warm breeze passed across his face, fatigue set in. His journey had taken too much out of him. He felt sleep approaching and his eyelids drooped. The light dwindled and the alien sounds of the camp began to fade, gradually replaced by sounds he could recognize, sounds once very familiar. He began to hear horses, a troop of horses, as it was when he was a young cavalryman, and they were drawing closer.

He could hear the laughter of men now, strong young men like he was once, and he heard them slow to a halt. He realized he was dreaming and his dream was of dusty summer roads, of bugle calls, of long journeys on horseback, and the memories came back welcome as old friends.

In his dream, he could see the boys grinning and jostling each other in their impatience to ride out and he could see his horse saddled and waiting, just like it was so many years ago. But he could not join them. In the dream he was still an old man. He wanted to ride away, to turn once more into the dust that swirled up around the troop, but they were young and he was old and he had forgotten the last time he was on a horse.

"Come on out, William," he heard them call. "Let's ride."

"Come on, Wee-yum," they teased. "Come out and play."

He could see faces that he remembered: faces of boys who rode with him through the steaming heat of an Atlanta summer or the brutal cold of Virginia during that last winter as the War finally began to wind down. He wanted to leave his chair, but could not move. He could speak to them though, and he happily replied.

"I can't go yet, boys," he said. "I wish I could. It won't be long, though. It won't be long."

"Well, damn it all, Wee-yum," they protested. "We gonna have some fun."

The old man wished he could go; he so wished he could go.

"Waal, we'll be back. We'll leave you your horse," they shouted laughingly as they wheeled around to the open road. "Just don't take the whole God damn day," they said as they rode away. "You can catch up when you're ready."

After they left, he could see a horse standing patiently in the mud of the unfinished street in front of his son-in-law's new house. Although he knew better, he could have sworn it was the same young mount that threw him all those years ago, the one he returned to after he left the hospital, the one he finally broke and saddled and rode off on. Of course, it could not be; that horse had fallen at Kennesaw Mountain, shot through the lungs with its lifeblood pouring through its flared nostrils in its death spasm. But this was a dream, he reminded himself. It could be the same animal. Such things are possible in dreams.

The old man's heart began to pound, much as it did when he was young, when the world lay just beyond the Green River; when the troop paused at the ford and looked at the water, knowing that when they rode across they would be part of a great army with a grand noble purpose. He would be part of history; he knew that, and he could feel the weight of his duty pressing down on him.

Then he noticed something, but said nothing, since it was only a dream and he knew it was a dream and a dream of long ago at that. As the boys rode away, laughing and singing in the clean untested splendor of their youth, he could see that some of them wore the dusty blue uniform of the North and some wore butternut, or the faded gray tunic of the South.

Sally's in the Garden

"Where are all these people comin' from, Aunt Malissy?" Rissie asked as they walked through the town. "I didn't think they were that many people in the world."

The crowd was moving slowly toward the bridge over Greasy Creek. On the other side, along the railroad tracks that followed the creek, a larger crowd had already gathered. Rissie could hear music from a brass band playing songs she had never heard before, but she remembered that, until McKinney Steel built the town, she had never heard a brass band. Somehow, the incessant roar of the town, built around the great mine and its machinery, had abated. In the intervals between the music, she could hear birds. The McKinney Steel Company had stopped all work for this occasion.

Also in those intervals, she could hear other music as well. As she turned the corner of the Greasy Creek Hotel, she found three young men playing a banjo, a fiddle and a mandolin just as energetically as the company band was puffing into its horns. A small crowd had gathered around the boys, and although she could not see them clearly, she thought she recognized something in the banjo chords that arched over the murmurs of the crowd.

I know who that is, she thought. I've heard that before.

Her heart quickened, as they followed the crowd across the bridge to the railroad tracks.

It was a special day, and Rissie had walked down from Gardner Fork to Malissa Prater's house. There was a ceremony to be held and speeches to be made. Malissa wanted Rissie to attend the festivities with her and Rissie was happy to be asked. Both she and Malissa loved each other's company, and both were a little bewildered at what had happened so rapidly to Greasy Creek.

It was difficult for Rissie to comprehend that such change had come to her isolated creek, that a train now huffed and puffed its way into Greasy Creek's heart. She remembered Mammy's tales of the first train, but it was nothing like these monstrous black beasts. Neither could she believe that men still disembarked from them every day, looking for and easily finding work. Where once lay cornfields below the forks of Greasy Creek, new houses now pressed shoulder-to-shoulder and crowded against brand-new concrete sidewalks. A real town had sprung up here, seemingly overnight. *A town! A real town! On Greasy Creek!* She was just a little frightened at what had happened to her valley. As the first houses went up, row on orderly row of two-story clapboard structures, Rissie wondered how they would ever fill them all with people, but the waiting list for company housing filled rapidly and diminished only as new houses were completed.

Where they all comin' from?

Until the camp houses were built, all up and down Greasy Creek accommodations were made to house the new workers for the mine. Farm children grumbled as they were packed even more tightly, four or more to a bed, with their siblings so that a room could be turned over to boarders. The demand for a place to sleep was unbelievable. In a very few cases, whole families moved into converted sheds or smokehouses to permit the house to accept paying guests.

Even then, that was not enough; men who could find no place to stay streamed across the mountains daily from neighboring creeks to work in the Greasy Creek mine. Malissa shook

shook her head in response to Rissie's question; she had never seen anything like this either.

"Hell, honey, there ain't no end to the people in the world," she replied. "But I'm like you: I never thought I'd see the day there'd be this many on Greasy Creek."

Malissa herself had strangers living under her roof. After her husband, Daniel Jack Prater, died of typhoid in 1914, their large house emptied as her children grew up and moved away. She opened her house to borders, as much for the company as for the money, and only on the recommendation of her son Peter or IB Sanders. Her first boarder, Grafton Willoughby, came from Western Kentucky and was a carpenter. He first lived in the tent city that sprang up when the mine opened, but IB Sanders had vouched for him and that was good enough for Malissa. Although Grafton had moved into one of the houses he built with his wife and family, Malissa still visited the Willoughbys in their new quarters nearly every day. IB had recommended well; Malissa became close to the family.

IB was like a brother-in-law to Malissa, since Daniel Jack Prater, her husband, had been raised in the same house with IB. It happened after the War, when Rhoda Sanders, IB's mother, left her husband to marry Ezekiel Prater. Somewhat like Elisha Hopkins with his wives, Ezekiel kept his first wife and his children nearby and married her again after Rhoda's death. The Civil War had changed the social order of Greasy Creek dramatically and now the town would change it even more.

Rissie thought it odd to see new faces at Aunt Malissy's table, where the huge Prater clan once crowded together to take their meals, but now even some of Malissa's grandchildren were marrying. With jobs plentiful, there was little reason for young people to wait anymore, and children became adults with little transition. It was not like it was in the old days, and it bothered Malissa, whose pantries were always filled with canned food from her gardens, that these young people devoted so little time to learning how to keep house and plan for the future.

What if something happens to this God damn mine? These babies don't hardly know how to hoe a row of corn.

It was much the same at Rissie's house. All her brothers and sisters were marrying and leaving. Not two years before, her mother had finally succumbed to the effects of Spanish Influenza, a year after it had devastated Greasy Creek and sickened her, but within a month of her death, two of her children married. She wondered if people had already forgotten the Flu. So many had died then, or become invalids like her mother, wheezing and shivering and coughing up so much blood that it seemed her body could not replace it fast enough. She was never the same after she became ill, and she knew her time was short.

Barely more than a week after her death, her brother Bud had married, and within a month, Frank had married as well. (It was none too soon for Frank; his first child was born the following January). Now, two years later, they were raising their own families. It had nothing to do with lack of respect. It was Lila's wish that they would not wait. She wanted her children to marry and not let grief keep them from their new lives. It sounded cruel, Rissie thought, to marry in such haste, but haste was nothing anyone on Greasy Creek would have taken notice of as boys and girls were marrying right and left.

Frank and Manie Ethel made their home in one of the camp houses and it was hard for Rissie to spend more than a day away from them, especially since her new nephew had come along the previous year. Daybreak often found her limping down the Gardner Fork road to take fresh milk to Warren G. Harding Hopkins, whose strong feet and whole mouth gave such delight to his crippled aunt. He was named for the President, and could grow up to be one himself.

It still bothered Rissie that there had not been more time to grieve for her mother, but she understood the forces at work on Greasy Creek and all over the mountains. Mammy, her beloved grandmother, had taught her how to accept the things she could not change, whether in the world she grew up in or the body she could not outgrow. Rissie knew that she would never be like the shy young brides she saw getting off the train, furtively seeking their new husbands amid the tumult of the overcrowded depot, but she was happy for them, as they recognized each other and marched off to their new homes in the Upper or Lower Camp. There was even talk of a third camp in the broad field at the forks where long ago Elisha Hopkins kept horses and the clan gathered every summer to celebrate its success, although few on Greasy Creek could remember that time. Elisha had been gone for seventeen years and most of the collective memory the creek had of the old man was limited to his cursing young boys who threw rocks at his house and that was nearly forgotten. Few people chose to remember him anymore; few chose to remember anything of the life that was there before the mines came.

Rissie knew the past was slipping away, but she was glad that her family and her friends found the men or women they would spend the rest of their lives with. She could have felt abandoned as they all turned to their new lives, but she did not, or would not. She knew, as did everyone, that her fate was to take care of her broken-hearted father until he died, since the possibility of her marrying was so remote. No one would say that aloud; she also knew. With what life had handed her, she needed no reminders of her disabilities.

The new town of Greasy Creek was awash in strong, handsome young men, but none were interested in Rissie; the town was also swimming in young women who were not afflicted with Rissie's limp and crooked smile. It would have been a competition she could not win, and she wisely avoided even hoping for a man.

Rissie's closest friends were the old people of Greasy Creek instead of the young, as her childhood friends relentlessly left her side. With few friends her own age, she became much the surrogate daughter to widows whose own children had grown up and departed, and Rissie's mother was neither the first nor would be the last to look into her kind eyes as she took her last breath, and Rissie accepted her role. It was undeniable that Greasy Creek and, indeed, all of Pike County had changed, and the opportunities of the present had nearly destroyed the obligations to the past.

"You know, Sissy," Malissa said reflectively as they turned the corner past the Greasy Creek Hotel, "I can remember when they built that old logging camp over there before you was even born." Malissa pointed to what was now a lot filled with nine identical houses, with nearly all their tiny yards filled with screaming children and clothes drying on lines strung across the porches. "We couldn't hardly believe that so many people would come to Greasy Creek then and now look at this place. Your mammy cooked for them, since the camp was so close to her house. Boys and girls used to meet at her house at the end of the week."

Malissa stared at the crowded field and slowly shook her head. "We had some good times in that house," she said.

But the old house was gone, although somewhere under the new concrete and plaster and wood of all the new houses might still be the scattered rocks that formed its foundations, but no one who lived there now would have reason to remember it. Most of them had never heard of Greasy Creek before they came for the work. Perhaps only Rissie and a few of the old people of the creek could still see the house in its weathered glory. It was a magical place for the young people of Greasy Creek in its hey-day, and there would never be anything like it again.

"I remember it too," said Rissie wistfully. Her father wanted to buy it after Mammy's death, but he was stilly paying for the place on Gardner Fork. *I wish I could go back there, she thought. I wish Mammy was still here and I wish I could stay with her forever.*

Up ahead, a large crowd had formed directly on the railroad tracks and the band ceased playing as a smartly dressed gentleman moved to the edge of the loading dock, now hastily cleared of the usual piles of boxes and crates that were unloaded daily from the trains. The new school built by the company had closed for the day and the students were lined up beside the tracks in newly pressed clothes, waiting for the speakers to begin. The trains kept back at a respectful distance as the music ended and the ceremony finally began. The workers had been called out of the pits and Rissie could see them laughing and jostling each other as young men do when given an unexpected leave from hard work. She strained to find her brother Frank among the uniformly black faces of men who spent their days in darkness and danger under the mountains she played on as a child and where she still tended the graves of her family.

She could not see him in the small army of dust-covered men, but she knew he was there. If she had to, she could find her brother in the dark.

It was spring when Frank Hopkins left the Army and came back to Greasy Creek, early spring, when the fields were just dry enough to plow and farmers were inspecting their seed corn to make sure the mice have not robbed too much of it over the winter. He had been surprised to see many fields lying fallow, but he realized that the men who would have been planting were now working in the mines, making enough money to buy food instead of raising it. It was an odd sight to Frank, who had always worked the fields with his father, who taught him well that a man's first priority was make sure his family had enough to eat.

Harrison was mistrustful of all the new wealth, and when his sons came back, he handed them their old overalls, washed and pressed by their mother, to replace the Army uniforms they had worn home. Once again they began walking behind Daisy, Harrison's venerable gray mule, to lay off the gardens they had left barely a year before. Frank was still not able to fully comprehend what he had been through and was thankful that Daisy was still alive and that he had a routine to return to, but he was restless. He knew he could find work in the mines anytime he wanted; anyone who wanted a job could have one. But in April of 1919, he was a farm boy again, although what he wanted most was his own house and a family.

Now two years later, he had both, even if the house was merely rented. He was supremely happy.

Harrison knew that as soon as his boys came home they would marry. His oldest child, a daughter, had already married and had children of her own. He knew Frank and Bud were looking for places to live before Lila died, but he cautioned them to wait a while longer. By contrast, Lila encouraged them to go ahead; it may have been that she knew her time was short, and she wanted to see her boys happy. They had real jobs now, and were making good money, but Harrison had no confidence that the mine would last and he worried that they would go into the pits and never return. He tried to impress the danger on Frank and Bud, who had gone off to fight the Kaiser and survived, but both his sons felt nothing could harm them again.

"Get your garden out f-first," Harrison told the boys, sputtering as he always did with his unrepaired cleft palate. "Then get you a job and save your m-money. The way they're dying in that m-mine, there'll be p-plenty of jobs."

Harrison was right about the death toll of the Greasy Creek mine. It was no more dangerous than any other mine, and in fact, safety was a great priority of McKinney Steel, but it had already claimed several lives. Most of the Greasy Creek boys attributed the deaths to the demands made on the mine when it had too few men to work and too much demand for coal for the war effort. Now that the war was over and the mine improving every day with new equipment, it would soon be the safest mine in Pike County. Price McKinney wanted it to be the safest mine in the world.

Unlike the mines over in West Virginia, Greasy Creek's mine was a blessing: it had no methane gas, which killed so many men in explosions on the other side of the Tug River, the Big Sandy's smaller sister. The disaster at Monongah, West Virginia in 1907 was still talked about, but Greasy Creek's deaths came mostly from roof falls, sudden collapses of the top where the men dug coal out of the great seams of Greasy Creek or in the tunnels on the way to the face of the seams where they worked. Since the war ended, the bosses felt less pressure and constantly preached safety, so the Greasy Creek boys felt safe enough to marry, and safe enough to plan out their lives around mining coal.

Frank knew full well that he too could die in the mines, but discounted the likelihood, at least not anytime soon. He did, however, tell Manie what he wanted at his funeral, should the worst happen. Unless that happened, he would put in his time and collect his pay, and he constantly reassured his wife and his father that he was in no danger.

Still, Harrison maintained that a garden was an absolute necessity. He had never failed to make sure his family had food when snow was on the ground, even in the hard times following the Civil War, when he was a child and often had to sit up at night with a gun to protect the hogs from neighbors who had none. Nearly everyone on Greasy Creek was starving in those years. Hungry bellies often drove their owners to desperation.

Harrison had always done his chores without complaint, and his boys, as long as they lived under his roof, would have to do theirs, whether they became rich coal miners or not. He had never in his life seen as much money as his sons brought home every week and he worried they would forget what it meant to be frugal. Harrison trusted his mule, his corn, his hogs and his bees; he did not trust the roaring, steaming, snorting thing that covered the valley of his birth and drowned out the sounds of the birds. And he grieved for the fields he once worked, now covered with houses and children and laundry drying in the sooty air.

But Harrison knew change had to come. His garden was smaller this year, since he did not have Lila, and every year another of his children married and moved away from home. When Frank came up on weekends to help his father, he had little heart in it, and it wasn't merely because his beloved mother no longer walked the earth. His wife and child were now his greatest priorities.

Frank was happy where he was; he was making money and could now afford a few things for the house, which was Manie Ethel's pride. With the oversight of her mother and her grandmother, Granny Rebecca Damron, she made new curtains and quilts and Frank had bought her a new cook stove, which was nearly paid off. Manie stretched every penny and studied ways to save more: she kept wood splinters in a bowl on the mantel above the fireplace so Frank would not need matches when he wanted to smoke. She cleaned the globes of the kerosene lamps every day so the light would not be hindered and there would be no need to turn up the flame. She avoided using the electricity, although the cost was a flat rate deducted from Frank's payday; she simply did not want to take the chance of blowing a bulb and having to replace it.

She made a home for her husband and child and prayed every day that Frank would come home unhurt. He worked long, hard hours and was weary, but he was happy with his life. He missed his mother and would miss her forever, and he would soon have enough money for a proper tombstone for her lonely grave on the Old Prater Cemetery.

You have to take what life hands you, he thought, but life is pretty good. Frank could still smile in April of 1921.

*   *   *

Price McKinney was furious. For nearly a year now, from the time Jimmy Corrigan received full control of his forty percent of the McKinney Steel Company, Corrigan had bedeviled the older man, his former trustee, and now he had gone so far as to file a lawsuit against him and his management of the company.

"The sheer audacity..." McKinney muttered to himself as he read the papers a courier had just delivered. He took off the thick, round trademark eyeglasses he wore, the result of diminishing sight from pouring over thousands of account books and repeated, "The sheer audacity!"

One of the charges young Corrigan had made was that McKinney had no right to change the name of the company. For years now, Corrigan had seethed that McKinney had amended the formal name of Corrigan, McKinney and Company to McKinney Steel Company. It did not matter that McKinney's partners were dead and he had single-handedly increased the fortunes of their heirs beyond all expectations or that he had a national reputation and the ear of Presidents; the man simply had no right to drop his father's name from the company he created. The claim was among a litany of minor slights that Jimmy felt he had suffered (or Laura Mae, his wife, told him he had suffered) under the man who had signed millions of dollars in dividend checks to him.

McKinney saw no problem with changing the name of the company: Captain Jim Corrigan was gone, McKinney had saved the company from bankruptcy nearly thirty years before, and Jimmy Corrigan certainly would never run it. As for his management, McKinney's salary was much less ostentatious than most captains of industry, which he could easily prove in court, and every shareholder benefited handsomely from his work. And besides, the courts would share McKinney's absolute lack of respect for the son of his former partner and friend, who trusted his own son so little that he would not allow him control of his legacy until he turned forty!

Young Corrigan and his upstart wife, who was both a former waitress and a divorcee, were never part of Cleveland society, which remembered well the gossip surrounding Jimmy's many affairs. They remembered the messy lawsuit that the young man faced when he broke off an engagement with a Pittsburgh socialite, and the shocking stories that swirled around his famous parties, where he met a ravishing Laura MacMartin, nee Whitlock, wife of a socially acceptable, but financially limited

Chicago doctor. Considering his previous foibles, it was only a minor shock to Cleveland society when Laura filed for divorce and married Jimmy before the ink had fully dried on her divorce decree.

When invitations to a reception for the new couple at the Corrigan estate were not returned, they knew that old-money Cleveland families would simply shut them out, and the pair moved to New York, where Laura would have more success. That she had, only to a degree, however. She found a member of the old aristocracy, now of limited financial means, to sponsor her, and after spending a small fortune to influence New York society with only minimal results, the couple moved on to London, where she became hugely successful in her quest. Her boundless wealth finally impressed the remnants of the aristocratic families who had lost so much during the war.

McKinney hoped they would stay there and, for the most part, Laura did, but Jimmy was returning more and more often to Cleveland, to McKinney's growing annoyance. McKinney had no use for the aging playboy and very much preferred that he follow the same routine he had observed since his father died: stay away, cash the dividend checks, and let McKinney run the company as he always had.

Jimmy Corrigan had demanded and gotten an office and a secretary at company headquarters in the Perry-Payne Building, but he had no duties and was deliberately kept out of every management decision McKinney made. Jimmy was the single largest shareholder in the company except for McKinney, and by McKinney's orders, most of the headquarters staff ignored him. Captain Jim's son was never given access to McKinney's inner sanctum, where his father and McKinney had begun an empire, after a fateful shouting match that Jimmy initiated and McKinney walked away from in disgust.

"Now this insolent pup would dare sue me?" McKinney said aloud as he re-read the papers for a second time. Things had

gone on long enough, he thought. This is completely unaccept-
able, the final straw. *The sheer audacity!*

But then a light went on in McKinney's mind: this lawsuit
actually could be useful, he thought. Jimmy Corrigan's con-
quests were only of women; he does not know either how to run
a steel company or the true role of an American industrialist.
Neither has he the respect I have in this city. I will fight him and
I will win and since I still have the proxy of Judge Burke's
family, I will remove him from the board of McKinney Steel
forever. Then young James W. Corrigan, Jr. may return to
Europe and his harlot wife with his tail between his legs and I
shall be done with him.

McKinney leaned back in his padded leather chair and relaxed: this was almost too easy. He was supremely confident of
his strategy; after all, he had defeated far greater enemies than
Jimmy Corrigan. He put his glasses back on and pressed the
buzzer to summon his secretary; it was time, once again, to
speak to his attorney.

The sheer audacity!

*   *   *

"A hundred years from now," said the speaker. "Greasy
Creek will look back to this day as the beginning of the greatest
period of prosperity in its existence. A new, fully-equipped
hospital is under construction, and new stores and buildings are
planned for the good people of this valley."

The speaker, whom Rissie did not know, went on to hint that
another whole camp might soon be built. She had heard the
rumors that Uncle Harmon's house would be sold to the company, just as his son Jeff's property and store had been, and
Elisha's old farm would soon be the location for even more
houses. Beside the speaker, on the cleared dock, were several
other men Rissie did not know, although she could not miss
Peter Prater in his best Sunday clothes. He stood near the back

of the platform, beside the American flag and a flag that she was told represented the McKinney Steel Company. Malissa pointed repeatedly with pride to her son, as if he was still in school, and grinned broadly when the speaker thanked him for his fine work in building the houses and buildings that created the town. Rissie was close enough to see the new, bleached-white concrete base of the tram with "1921" formed into it. Maybe this is a special year, she thought.

The tram had been built rapidly, but sturdily. It seemed to have crawled up the hillside nearly overnight; like a monstrous steel snake that grew as it moved, like everything else that happened so rapidly on Greasy Creek. It replaced the old chutes that carried coal down the mountain at such a speed that a large portion of it spilled over the top of the gondolas when they emptied into them. An entire crew of men had no other job but to shovel up the spilled coal and fling it back into the gons before they left Greasy Creek for Cleveland. It was just another wonder of the town; already there was electricity and steam heat for the bosses and a new post office, a telegraph office, and two company stores, plus another private store to attend to the needs of the miners. A new, grand commissary was planned for the town, where everything could be bought under one roof. It was a real town, growing by leaps and bounds every day.

It seemed to Rissie, and was confirmed by her brothers, that this was the most modern coal mine in the world. Maybe soon, the deaths would cease and even injuries would be a thing of the past. Rissie wondered if Mammy had been as impressed when the little narrow-gauge railroad was built thirty years before to haul the trees out of Greasy Creek.

She still wondered what Greasy Creek had been like when the great trees were still there. Like most of the young people of the creek, she could remember only what she had been told about the time before the mine came. There was little else to remind her.

Eventually, the speeches ended and the band played a final patriotic song before the crowd moved off the track, and even before it had fully retired, the gondolas began backing up the tracks in anticipation of receiving the first glistening black fruit of the miners' labors from the perpetual motion of the giant, soulless thing that had just been consecrated by the company. As the first load fell loudly into the waiting car, the crowd clapped and cheered.

After the ceremony, Malissa and Rissie turned toward the center of town to pay a visit to the Willoughbys. Mary Jane Willoughby, the daughter of the old soldier who had come to Greasy Creek the year before, had invited them to come by their house. Now that her husband Grafton's carpentry job was just about done, they would soon move back to Western Kentucky, but they were not sure if the old man would be going with them.

The old Union soldier, who had come to Pike County as a young man so long ago that he could barely remember it, was dying.

As they crossed the bridge back to the center of town, Rissie could hear music again. Up ahead, on a corner across from the Greasy Creek Hotel, a young crowd had gathered around the source. Rissie could hear the song:

> *Sally does your dog bite, No sir no.*
> *Daddy cut his biter off a long time ago.*
> *Sally's in the garden, sifting, sifting*
> *Sally's in the garden, sifting sand.*

"I believe that's the boy," Malissa said.

Rissie knew she had to be talking about Harlen, now fifteen years old and, in spite of his age, by all standards the handsomest man on Greasy Creek. He was two years younger than Rissie, but every young girl on Greasy Creek, regardless of her age, wanted him for her beau.

"Let's speak to him," said Malissa. "Then we got to get on over to the Willoughbys. They say old man Bracken is pretty bad off."

Harlen was playing his banjo low on his hips when he saw Rissie approach and he raised it up on his chest and smiled at her. Rissie thought for a moment that he had raised it so she could not avert his eyes and would have to look at him.

He wants me to look at him, she thought. With his big shoulders and perfect teeth, every girl looks at him. Why would he want to look at me?

Their song ended and Malissa charged through the crowd with Rissie in tow.

"Howdy, Aunt Maliss," Harlen said. "You come down for the speeches?"

"Hell, no," she grinned. "I just wanted to see that damn thing fall down when they started it up. But it didn't. How's your mommy and daddy?"

"They're doin' very well," he answered, but when he spoke he was looking at Rissie.

Why is he looking at me? Everybody else is looking at him.

"What you want to hear?" Harlen asked his great aunt. "I'll play anything you want."

Once again, when he spoke, he was looking not at Malissa, but directly at Rissie. Her face reddened and she was certain everyone could see her. It did not please her to blush; it would only cause her more humiliation.

"We got to be going," Malissa said. "You tell your folks I been thinkin' about 'em."

"Yes, Ma'am, I will."

As Malissa walked up the street toward the Willoughby's home, Rissie was right behind her and just before they stepped up on the porch, she turned just enough to take a final look at the street corner where Harlen was playing.

He was still watching her, and he smiled when he saw her blush again.

After they finished, one of his partners kneeled down to count the pennies and nickels that had been thrown into the fiddle case in front of them. To his displeasure, Harlen noticed one of the boys in the crowd making a snorting sound as he raised his upper lip. Not only that, but the young man began to exaggerate a limp as he walked around a small group of giggling girls. Harlen's face reddened dangerously.

"Hey, boy," he said as the young man stopped his dance. "Did you put any money in Billy's case?"

"Hell no, Harlen," the boy replied. "I ain't got no money."

"Well, good," said Harlen, as he stomped the offender's foot with the heel of his boot and then followed up with a mighty fist to his lips. The boy barely had time to feel the pain of his broken tarsi before everything went black. Later, he would walk home with a limp and a split lip in a close approximation of the infirmities of the little girl he had mocked.

"I wouldn't want to have to give it back," Harlen said as he picked up his banjo and walked away.

*   *   *

She had not known the old man as well as she wanted to. There were things he would talk about, if she asked him, but when he spoke it was not for long, as he tired quickly. He would answer a question or two, but when she asked another, she would find him sleeping and she would not take him from his rest. She knew a few things about him: he had been a soldier, a Union soldier, but he harbored no ill will toward the Confederates he fought. And indeed, when he died, the sons of former Confederate soldiers made his coffin and lowered him into his grave. Sarah, his wife, had been gone over twenty years and until he died, he still felt the pain of her leaving. His son had gone down on the *Titanic,* along with the last of the old man's fortune. Now none of his family would sleep near him: his wife rested in Muhlenberg County where she died in 1898, and he would rest here, in Pike County, as far away as he could get from her and still be in Kentucky.

And their son was somewhere on the bottom of the Atlantic Ocean. It made Rissie shiver.

There ain't no good way to die, she thought, but that must have hurt Mr. Bracken something awful.

Perhaps that was why the old man spoke so little about the past: he was still trying to make sense of it as he lay on his deathbed. It was as if he came to Greasy Creek in twilight and remained there until the darkness enveloped him. All around him were the living, but closest to him were ghosts: the ghost of his wife, of his son, of his comrades on dusty fields a half-century before, of the fine horses he had shod, of the horses he had rode into battle, of the horses with broken legs and shattered bodies he put out of their misery with a bullet. He had been a blacksmith and a farmer, honorable professions, and he had been an honorable man, and he had come to Greasy Creek to die.

At his funeral, Rissie wept, not because it was not his time, because in truth it was, but because it was not his place. Although his family was assured that his grave would not be neglected, that it would always be tended and honored, Rissie could see their apprehension, and the guilt they bore because they could not take him home. He would sleep forever among the Hopkinses and the Praters, who were not strangers, but still not family. He would sleep not far from her mother's grave, but there would be no dust of his own nearby.

The old man would tell Rissie no more stories, tell her nothing further of his life. She had Mammy's stories she still fiercely protected, but now she had the unknown stories of the old Union soldier she could not tell, and she wept for the loss. Mammy had taught her that all family stories are precious.

But with the family gone, to whom would she tell the old man's stories even if she knew them? The Willoughbys would soon be leaving Greasy Creek and moving back to Western Kentucky, although one of the Willoughby boys would stay on in Eastern Kentucky and one of the Willoughby girls, would stay with Malissa for a while longer. She was in love and Mary Jane had given her permission to marry, but only when Aunt Malissa thought it proper. Alta Willoughby was only thirteen, Rissie thought. Would she ever want to know what her grandfather did in the War?

Grafton was growing sicker by the day; his asthma had worsened and soon he would no longer be able to work. The Willoughbys had to return to their own place, where they could raise a garden and live simply to help make ends meet. Mary Jane trusted Malissa to look out for her daughter and take care of her father's grave. There was simply no way they could afford to embalm him and send his body on the long journey back to Muhlenberg.

But there was beauty in the funeral, and symmetry. The preacher was Uncle Bob Damron, who had ridden with the old man over a half-century ago, although neither man actually remembered the other, and there was IB Sanders, the son of a Confederate soldier and the brother of another Confederate soldier who did not come home, who handled the final affairs of William Bracken for the family. Two other Union soldiers slept nearby, comrades of Uncle Bob and unremembered comrades of the old man. *They'll stand guard with him, Rissie thought. That's what soldiers do.*

It was now the second of May; the old man had died on the last day of April, the same month Rissie was born. So many things had happened in April: her brothers, Bud and Frank, came home in April. The twins, Bessie and Jessie, who were Harrison and Lila's last children, were born in April. She also allowed herself to remember that Harlen Damron had been born in April, but she wasn't sure why she should. And there were other, bigger things that happened in April: the *Titanic* had gone down in April; the country went into war with the Kaiser in April; and in yet another April so long ago, the country went to war with itself.

She wondered what future Aprils would bring.

"You comin' with us, girl?" Malissa asked her, as the mourners filed out of the cemetery. "I got dinner on the table."

"I'll be along directly, Aunt Malissy," Rissie said. "I think I'll stay here a little longer."

"You be careful walkin' down that hill then."

Rissie watched the men fill and mound the old man's grave under IB's supervision. He smiled at her as the men collected their tools and departed. Soon she was alone on the cemetery again. She could see the honeysuckle growing along the fence, although it was still too early for it to bloom. In her mind, she recommended it to the old man.

You'll like this, Mr. Bracken, when it blooms. There ain't no sweeter smell than honeysuckle. This is your land now too, and you'll probably see your great-grandchildren down at the school one of these days. Your granddaughter'll marry soon and your blood will go on.

We'll take care of your grave. Aunt Malissy said so and I say so. I'm sorry you couldn't go home to your wife, but you'll see her, maybe you see her right now.

In the distance, the noise of the town continued unabated. The shrill whistle of the locomotive, the loud hiss of its brakes as it stopped, the mightier hiss of the power plant in town, the rattle of the tram bearing its cargo down the mountain, and the chatter of the people all rode the wind up the hill to the cemetery. *It don't stop, she thought. It don't never stop.*

The old man had not died in the Greasy Creek mine, so there was no reason for it to stop. For that matter, even when someone was killed, which was often, the sounds of the mine and the town only paused. There was no reason to stop for funerals, Rissie thought, and no time for funerals anymore; nobody even has time to live. Death is just an aggravation.

What was it like when death meant something, Mammy? Was it really the way you told me it was? Was it truly different, all those years ago? Would anybody even care anymore?

123

Birds were chirping in the cemetery as Rissie closed and locked the gate behind her, and it made her smile in spite of her sadness. She looked back at the cemetery a final time before making her descent and found comfort in its isolation.

Up here, she thought, nothing would ever change.

Babylon Summer

"It wouldn't that bad," the old men would tell me, when I asked them what it was like to work in the Greasy Creek mine. "Men got killed all the time, but it wouldn't as bad as some other mines." And they would add, "The company paid good, too." In spite of the acknowledged death toll, I never heard an unfavorable comment about the company that owned the mine and the town of Greasy Creek. "They were good to us," the men agreed.

Generally speaking, steel companies followed more closely the philosophy of the Progressive Era than the coal companies, who competed to produce the cheapest coal to sell on the open market. The steel companies usually paid better and offered more benefits, such as health care for the miner and his family. They also felt a cultural responsibility. Recreational and social opportunities were created and schools were built, where children usually received a far better education than their counterparts in the politics-ridden local school districts surrounding the camps. But by and large, men came to Greasy Creek or any of the camps for the money.

"All I asked of my men was what the company asked of me," my great-grandfather Peter Prater said on his deathbed in 1980. "A good day's work for a good day's pay." He was rambling when he spoke to me, the result of a poor oxygen supply to his brain, but he was still lucid enough to talk about the past. He was dying from pneumonia in a Pikeville hospital as a result of its refusal to change his medication without permission from

Peter's doctor, whom the hospital staff could not find after he admitted my great-grandfather and disappeared on a drunken toot.

His sons and I wrestled with him constantly before he died, holding his arms to keep him from getting out of bed in his delirium, as none of us wanted to see him strapped down. I was furious at the hospital staff for the neglect, but the hospital was another typical Pike County political system and patients were considered chattel of the doctors. It was another reason why I hated the place of my birth; politics were part and parcel of growing up in the coal fields. My great-grandfather was 102, but he was still too young to die, and for the first time in my life, I truly listened to what he had to say. I knew those would be the last things he would tell me.

"A good day's work for a good day's pay," he repeated, with an element of pride in his weakening voice. "That was what the company believed, and that was what I believed." There was no doubt what Peter Prater believed.

"I had to fire Andrew once or twice," he chuckled, remembering my grandfather as a boy. "He was always asking to run an errand somewhere to get off the job. Andrew wasn't all that partial to hard work, you know, but I always let him come back. He had those children..." One of them was my mother.

During his last intervals of lucidity, I realized there was so much more I could have learned had I taken the time, but it was too late. Perhaps my rage at the hospital included the rage I felt at myself for waiting so long to ask him about the past and to follow through on the promise I had made Ed Ratliff twenty years before.

My great-grandfather told me he was surprised when IB showed him the plans for the Greasy Creek camp and discovered the measures the company had taken to ensure the health of the miners. One of them was that toilets would be built of concrete and would regularly be cleaned out. There was a reason for this: the houses had community wells and the company made sure that the cold, clear water that Greasy Creek was known for would not be contaminated by effluent from the primitive 1920's sewage system. Greasy Creek had lost its trees twenty years before, but the groundwater was still pure, at least when the camps were built.

Bacteriology was in its adolescence when Price McKinney built the Greasy Creek camp and its sister operation at Wolfpit, and penicillin was forty years away, but his insistence on good conditions for his men and their families saved lives. Manie Ethel's uncle Lonnie Coleman, his wife, and four children died of typhoid during one devastating epidemic in the summer of 1924, but they did not live in the camps. Communicable diseases stalked the mountaineers increasingly as open space between farms disappeared. Typhoid had taken Peter's father's life in 1914 and the disease was not unusual, but ten years later it ravaged whole families.

The McKinney Steel Company took an active role in fighting it the summer the Coleman family was devastated. The company doctor and his nurses went to every home in the camps, inoculating families and instructing miners' wives on sanitation. The company regularly sent home instructional health flyers with the men who did not live there. The 1924 epidemic raged, but the Greasy Creek camp largely escaped the plague because the medicines were effective and, in part, because the toilets were regularly cleaned out.

The fact that there would be jobs other than mining, service jobs at the camp, was something new for the mountaineers who had lived much by barter since the Civil War. They knew there were timber men who set the timbers that supported the roof, and brattice men who hung the curtains that directed fresh air to the mine face, and track layers who extended the internal rail system as the coal seam retreated. But there were other jobs that were new to them: machine runners, trip riders, mechanics and electricians. It was odd, they thought, to work in a coal mine and not actually mine coal.

One enterprising miner noticed that a sanitation job, commonly referred to as "honeydipper," had no takers when the duties were explained. He watched the wage offer rise steadily and when it reached the point that other miners talked about it, he signed up. He suffered the insults and derision of his fellow miners as long as he worked at his job, but in 1928 he had saved enough to purchase a grand two-story Sears home, which was shipped to Greasy Creek by rail and which included its own Delco electric generator. For twenty years, although he lived there for only two, it was the finest house outside the camps.

Still, most men wanted to load coal. The average pay for a timberman rose to over $7.00 a day by 1928, but the average price per ton paid to the miner for loading coal was $1.35. If, like Tennessee Ernie Ford sang, a man could load sixteen tons, he could make twice what a day laborer made. Even after deducting the cost of the explosives he used to blast the coal from the mountain and his tools for drilling into the seam, he could still carry home more money than any other classification. Considering the benefits the McKinney Steel Company provided, it was no wonder the men wanted to work at no other mine.

The reason for McKinney's insistence on improving miners' living conditions was not just altruistic: it ensured a stable workforce. The wholesome social activities he sponsored were also part of a plan to keep the miners away from drinking and fighting, which sometimes crippled mines on Monday mornings. Although alcohol was illegal—the Volstead Act had recently been passed—it was readily available, and too many of the men who spent their days in toil under the mountains looked for diversions on the weekend, after they had survived another week underground. So McKinney paid for a band, and supplied space in company buildings for clubs and chaperoned dances.

"We had about everything we needed," Rissie told me. "There was a movie theater, and they had dances at the hotel. There was a hospital with a good doctor. There was a church and a school, but we went to Middle Greasy School. That was a county school and we didn't have that much, but down in the camps they had all kinds of clubs. They had a band that played music on Saturday. The company even had a baseball team and we all went to the games. Woe be to any others that came to Greasy Creek and beat us."

She smiled when she recollected those days. "They'd just have to fight their way out."

Even then, murders and assaults were a natural by-product of the new availability of money and the old availability of alcohol. Both fueled egos and aggression, and Greasy Creek had its share of fisticuffs and shootouts. In one such battle, a deputy sheriff who was the son of a famous deputy sheriff of the Hatfield-McCoy feud died in a blaze of gunfire in front of the Greasy Creek Hotel, but not before shooting both of his assailants. Until the latest owner of the old building put up new vinyl siding, those bullet holes, along with others from lesser scrapes, were still visible.

Greasy Creek was not the only company town that offered a good day's pay for a good day's work, and it was not the only town that provided social services and recreational activities. That was not merely Price McKinney's vision for his corporation: other coal towns built by steel companies and a few of the larger coal companies followed that philosophy. But few company presidents threw themselves so whole-heartedly into improving the lives of his workers. His support of his company baseball teams was not limited to Cleveland. On more than one occasion, Greasy Creek miners were stunned to see the company president in their own bleachers, clapping and cheering as loudly as anyone.

The biggest problem for the Greasy Creek mine was the same problem all the camps faced: alcohol. Mountaineers were little affected by the Volstead Act; "stills" were as common after Prohibition as before, and miners had their thirsts quenched as easily as Main Line Clevelanders had Canadian Club discretely and regularly delivered to the back doors of their mansions.

Every two weeks, the miners would be paid, and before the weekend was over, Dr. Daniel Henry, the first company doctor on Greasy Creek, would have sewn up several knife, knuckle, or gunshot wounds, or pronounced some drunken miner dead. Drinking was as much of a hazard to the miners as the falling tops of the mines they worked in.

Although the steel industry suffered its ups and downs, the Roaring Twenties roared as loudly on Greasy Creek as anywhere. Price McKinney kept his men working full shifts every week, even when the economy slowed, which was not all that often. Machinery needed to be maintained, and coal could be easily stockpiled. The vast coke ovens near the McKinney Steel plant on the Cuyahoga River had huge black mountains that rose or fell, but the trains steadily unloaded and headed back to Kentucky for more.

The history of the coal industry is overshadowed by stories of labor strife, and it is difficult to conceive of a place where men were happy with their lot. Across the Tug River from Pike County, Matewan, West Virginia was the scene of an infamous shoot-out between Baldwin-Felts "detectives" and townspeople that left several dead, including the mayor and the brother of one of the Baldwin-Felts owners. The detectives had just finished another round of evicting striking miners and their families from the Stone Mountain Coal Company's houses, and the miners were fed up. When no convictions resulted from the battle, the detective agency responded by assassinating the Matewan police chief and his best friend a year later on the steps of the McDowell County, West Virginia courthouse. No one was prosecuted, and the injustice led to the Great West Virginia Mine Wars that culminated with US Army airplanes bombing coal miners at Blair Mountain to break the insurrection.

Greasy Creek experienced none of that. When I heard reminiscences of Greasy Creek from the men who worked there, it seemed as if it was perpetual summer, while in West Virginia or Harlan County, Kentucky, where the miners were abused and oppressed, the atmosphere seemed gloomy and cold. In every contemporary picture I have seen of these places, it seems to be winter.

When Frank Hopkins came back to the mines, the entry-level job that paid him $1.25 a day before the war now paid twice as much. Within a year, his wages doubled again. Eventually, he made nearly as much per hour as he had made per day before he went off to war. He purchased a pedal organ by mail and music lessons for Manie Ethel. Because she was often sick, it would give her something to do while she recuperated. As miners in Harlan County, Kentucky and Logan County, West Virginia dodged bullets, McKinney Steel employees perused Sears and Roebuck catalogs and walked out of the company store with Crosley radios. Talk of miners' unions on Greasy Creek was rare.

Price McKinney was not a believer in unions, since he felt that as long as every man was treated fairly, there would be no need for them. He had weathered a strike at the mill in 1919, but emerged from it with no union and still friends with his employees. His philosophy was accepted on Greasy Creek as well; I cannot remember a single soul who worked for McKinney Steel, or had a husband or father who worked there, who would tell me he was not treated as a man and did not receive a fair day's pay for a fair day's work. Indeed, that assessment could have been the result of the brief life of the Greasy Creek mine, but it was something the old men looked back on wistfully.

But even the good times had their dangers. The sudden accumulation of wealth, unknown to the mountaineers since before the Civil War, had its own problems.

"Nobody would save nothin'," said Rissie. "They'd spend it all like drunken sailors." (Although it is doubtful that Rissie ever saw a drunken sailor or the sea.) "Daddy would tell the boys to save their money and they'd go right out and spend it. I never saw so many of those old gas washing machines in my life as was lined up outside Luke Hamlin's store just before one payday. By Monday, every one of them was gone."

Not only Greasy Creek was prospering; the sheer excess of the Roaring Twenties affected all of Pike County. Automobiles were becoming available and the state and county governments began building roads. The old Mount Sterling-Pound Gap Road was rebuilt, and men began arriving in cars as well as trains or steamboats to take advantage of the work in Pike County. Probably none of them who drove that road, however, would have known that a heartsick former Vice President of the United States made the same journey as the Civil War broke out, and reluctantly traveled to his fate, like the miners now rushing blindly toward theirs. But John Cabell Breckinridge and the Confederacy, as well as the Cause itself, were long gone. Few people on Greasy Creek could remember them or worse, chose to. The seductions of the new age eclipsed the memories of all but a very few old soldiers and they were passing. During the half-century after the War, the heroes it produced had their stories kept alive by firelight and foxhunts, rituals across the mountains handed down through generations, but now it was over. The past had been largely abandoned because the present paid too well.

The county seat also boomed. New businesses in Pikeville opened every day, selling products that there would have been no market for a decade before. Almost anyone who wanted a job could find one and nearly anyone who started a business could reasonably count on success. Even the simplest entrepreneur could expect a return.

Boarding houses were common up and down the creeks and in the camps, and mostly catered to single men who worked in the mines. In Pikeville, there was a different clientele for many such establishments which were built to serve the many peddlers and hopeful businessmen who came through the region. As would be expected, access to a discrete bed often encouraged much more than sleep.

There was a lovely, marble stone in the Old Prater Cemetery, and until I grew up, Rissie would not tell me the story surrounding it, even when I asked her during our annual visits on Memorial Day. She would not tell me anything about it until I showed her a copy of a story in *The Pike County News* from 1924.

"Your Paw Pete bought that stone," she finally admitted. "He bought it for Hester. She was the most beautiful of all Aunt Malissy's girls and her man killed her. It just broke Malissy's heart."

She told me that Hester was married to Eli Adkins and he was not the kindest of husbands. He demanded she play the role of devoted wife and refused even to let her vote, although that was the law of the land since 1920. Instead, he expected her to keep up the house, raise the children, and run a boardinghouse to supplement their income. She had no need to vote, since women were born to be the servants of men, at least in Eli's reckoning. He had a business just downriver from Pikeville, and moved Hester and their children from Greasy Creek to Pikeville to take advantage of the higher room rates charged the businessmen who constantly streamed through the town. One of them was a peddler, a Lebanese immigrant who planned to open a dry goods store.

I also showed her an old picture of Melissa's family from 1920 and Rissie nodded her head in recognition. "That was Hester all right," she said. "She was a sweet girl."

The family had gathered in front of the Prater home for the funeral of Polly, Hester's older sister, and the picture showed both Hester and her husband on the porch, but oddly standing away from each other. The expression on Hester's face is certainly grief for her lost sister, but there may be as much grief for herself and for the loveless marriage she could not leave. By contrast, Eli's appears to be distant, immersed in ennui; it is easy to see that he would rather be somewhere else. He was a businessman and not a bad one, and he wanted to capitalize on any opportunity to make money. The funeral was taking him away from his work.

Hester was expected to do her part to make money, Rissie told me. As Eli's wife, she was responsible for maintaining decorum in the boardinghouse in addition to doing the cooking and the laundry. She was not expected to waste time receiving any kindnesses her life denied her.

"He didn't care any more for that woman than he did a draft horse," Rissie said, and she finally told me the story.

One day, Eli got up, had his breakfast, bade Hester good-bye and boarded the train for his job. However, as the train approached the outskirts of town, he disembarked at a small depot below the main station, walked back to his house, which he quietly entered and retrieved a long-barreled Colt .45. He found Hester supplying the Lebanese businessman with more than room and board, as he suspected he would, and pointed the revolver at the peddler's black hair. The bullet went into his brain and out his right eye, then traveled into Hester's left eye, lodging in the back of her skull.

Both died instantly. Eli was surprised he got them both with one shot.

He then calmly walked to the police station and brought the officers back to the bedroom where Hester was shown *in flagrante delicto*. He made no attempt to cover their nude bodies and was never prosecuted for the crime. The police, all of whom were his friends, gave a false story to the newspaper, reporting that Eli bravely defended himself against his whore of a wife and a deranged foreigner.

"He sent word up to Greasy for Peter and his brother Ike to come down there and get her," Rissie told me. "Eli wouldn't let his children come to the funeral and he never would let them decorate their mother's grave."

Eli went back to work the day after he killed his wife. He married again not long afterward. Peter buried his sister; bought her a marble column with an open Bible at its top, and life went on. Death, from blind violence, disease, or mining accidents was not uncommon in the hills.

Harmon Robinson's son, Caudill, died in a roof fall in the Greasy Creek mine and John, his brother, swore he would never work there or in any mine, but the lure of good wages was too much to resist. When John married Rissie's sister Bessie, who was only thirteen at the time, the young couple moved to neighboring Buchanan County, Virginia, where John took a job in the Harman mine.

"He said he thought he could work there since it had his daddy's name," Rissie said. "They spelled it different, but he didn't get killed."

Although death was always a real possibility, most miners accepted the risk; and the reality was that men died in Pike County nearly every day. In 1924, Rissie was saddened when Malissy told her that Asa Willoughby had died in a slate fall in a mine in Floyd County. Although Rissie wanted to go with Malissy to the funeral, she had to stay on Greasy Creek; she had other responsibilities by then.

Grafton and Mary Jane had gone back to Muhlenberg County two years before, but Asa, their oldest boy, had stayed in Eastern Kentucky because the wages were so much better than in the west. In fact, Jesse, their other son, had also returned to Eastern Kentucky to work.

Two years later, Rissie heard that Grafton Willoughby had died of his ancient illness. He had returned to Floyd County to tend to his dead son's final affairs, and stayed on because of the money. Again, Rissie could not go with Malissa to the funeral. By then she had even graver responsibilities: she was tending to her brother's son and he was dying.

*　　*　　*

Men died in the mines nearly every day, and Frank Hopkins worried about losing his life. He was not afraid of death; he had seen more lifeless, mangled bodies in one day in the Argonne than he would ever see on Greasy Creek and his worry was not for himself. He simply worried that there would be no one to take care of his family if he were killed.

Frank hoped to find a job by which he could make enough to leave the mines; he tried selling raincoats on the side and hoped he could build up his own business. He had no problems working for the McKinney Steel Company, but he knew all mines were deadly. Running a store was safe work and mining was like wartime: anyone could die at any time. The only difference was that the bodies could be recovered. He had seen men in the trenches completely disappear in deafening explosions; he had seen human bodies ground into the mud of the battlefield until they were unrecognizable as anything human. His grandmother had told him of the boys who went away from Greasy Creek in the Civil War and never returned, with no one knowing where they were buried or if they had a gravestone. He was terrified at the prospect of leaving his family nothing but a cold stone with nothing more than a name for his children to remember him by.

In 1927, he attended the funeral of Manie Ethel's grandfather Robert Damron, one of the last of the Civil War soldiers. He was almost ninety years old, and had been a preacher since he returned from service, horrified at the loss and destruction he had experienced. Frank and Manie Ethel had visited his house many times. Both his children had been born there, with Robert's wife Rebecca overseeing the midwives with sage advice. She had survived the Civil War and the stark years that followed and her nursing skills were legendary.

Frank shared a bond with the old man that eclipsed the fact that he married Robert's granddaughter: they had both shared the awesome experience of war. Both men had lived through it, survived, and came home to raise their families; both men had made their families their only reason for being.

Frank wept for the old man at his funeral, but Manie Ethel was not with him when Robert Damron was consigned to the earth and neither were his sons. He went there alone. His first son had been dead for six years and his wife had preceded her grandfather by four.

*   *   *

Of all the long-departed members of my family, there was only one soul that Rissie told me little about: Warren G. Harding Hopkins, my father's only brother, who was barely a year old when he died. Rissie had a wealth of information on my family and kept mental dossiers on people who had passed away as much as a half-century before she was born, but I could never elicit anything on Warren G. I attributed that to his death as an infant; one year is little time to beget memories and I thought there may not have been much to tell.

Yet I would wonder about him as I watched Rissie's eyes when she saw his tiny grave newly mounded on Decoration Day and she would steady herself to lean down and touch his small marble stone. When my father cleaned the grass and leaves off the graves—his responsibility as a son according to ancient mountain ritual—and step back to allow Rissie to push artificial flowers into the fresh dirt, I would compare their expressions.

In my father's face, there was still the confusion, the old tragedy of decorating graves of a mother and brother he never knew, but on Rissie's face, there was something else. She knew them and loved them; her grief was far more profound. After all those years, there was still the pain she had felt when she lost, cruelly and without warning, what had become her reason for living. It had never abated, and only my grandfather's expression was more piercing. I was never brave enough to speak to her about it.

After Rissie died in 1977, Laura Blackburn Hopkins, Frank's widow, called my brother up to her house. "You children need to have your grandmother's trunk," she said, and assigned him the task of removing it from the closet where it had rested for almost forty years. The grandmother she was referring to was neither she nor Rissie; none of us had known this grandmother. I had either forgotten or never knew the trunk existed, although my sister was allowed to play in it when she was a child. It was another opportunity I had missed to talk to my family. Although I was fascinated by what I found there, when I finally found time to peruse its contents it was too late to ask anyone about it. Both Rissie and Laura were gone.

Laura was my third grandmother. My brother and sister and I called her "Mammy," to differentiate her from "Mamaw" Rissie, who raised my father. Laura, who also descended from the infamous Elisha Hopkins through one of his four families, married Frank in 1929, six years after he lost his first wife and, as I gleaned from Rissie's stories, his mind and nearly any reason he had to live.

Laura had loved Frank her entire life, from the moment she first saw him on a Decoration Day long before World War I, when she climbed Ripley Knob with her father to decorate his father's grave. When she saw Frank arranging flowers there under the direction of his grandmother Dorcus, her heart pounded, and it had nothing with the long uphill walk to Elisha's cemetery. The Hopkinses, Robinsons, and Blackburns often made the trip before the mine came and destroyed the old road up to the cabin where Elisha had started his married life and where, seventy years later, he was buried.

Laura was Elisha's granddaughter and Frank was his great-grandson, but they knew little about each other growing up. Because of his many wives and children, Elisha was a common ancestor to many of the families of Greasy Creek. Laura was a pretty girl, with blond hair and a full figure, and had no lack of beaus, but she did not marry until she was twenty-five, old for any girl on Greasy Creek, which had few spinsters older than their teens. She did not know why she waited, but something told her not to accept any offer from any boy, regardless of his looks or his money.

It took many years for my grandmother Rissie to accept Laura; on that day on Elisha's cemetery, she could see how smitten Laura was with Frank and did not want her near him. She knew Frank was already taken, that even though he was still a boy, he loved Manie Ethel Coleman with all his heart and his love was more than reciprocated. Rissie knew they were made for each other, and did not want anyone to come between them, regardless of how pretty she was.

Rissie had no reason to worry. Frank barely noticed the young girl peeking out from behind her father as he spoke with the family. He was in a hurry. As soon as his father released him from his duties on Elisha's cemetery, he was leaving; he was having dinner at Manie Ethel's.

It did not take long for Laura to learn that she could never compete with the girl Frank loved so unreservedly. Although Laura was attractive, she had little else to offer. Manie came from a respected family, but Laura was the child of her father's second marriage, and some said he never married her mother. She knew few of her half-sisters and brothers from her father's first marriage. Some of Manie's aunts and uncles had college degrees and were teachers; Laura had never learned to read or write. Still, something told her to wait and she did.

I don't know why Mammy waited so long to give us the trunk; she may felt she was still competing with Manie Ethel after all those years. Maybe she was afraid that if my brother and sister and I had something tangible of our real grandmother, we would transfer the love we had for her to a ghost, but if we found it after her death we would not forgive her denying us some tangible record of the woman who birthed our father. Whatever the case, we were happy to get the trunk and when we opened it, one of the first objects we found was a rounded metal frame containing a laminated picture of an infant. Just below his oval picture were the words, "In Memoriam."

Warren G died of one of the many childhood diseases that swept through Pike County in waves as the hollows became more crowded. More houses meant more wells, depleting the groundwater that had always been abundant, as well as cold and pure; it also meant more outdoor toilets and contamination of that water. Summertime was always the most dangerous time, as mosquitoes flourished, adding an airborne threat to the waterborne pests and parasites. Children were especially vulnerable. When Warren G died in late July of 1921, Rissie had not had time to recover from the loss of her older sister Alice's two children two weeks before.

Rissie was ignored when the first children sickened; although she offered to tend them, her help was declined. What would a seventeen-year-old, who never had children and probably never would, know about sickness? She offered again when Warren G sickened and was again excluded. Once again, death visited the family. Rissie, in the grim determination she was capable of, swore she would never let that happen again.

In my grandfather's trunk was a small diary that held an entry from 1922, not long after my father was born: "Ethel in hospital in Huntington. Took out rib." From the time she had taken ill during the great Flu Epidemic, she was weakened, although she had successfully hidden her illness from Frank, at least before they were married. After Warren G died, she weakened further and when her second son was born, she began to fail. She had little milk for her son, who also became weak, and her chestnut hair seemed to lose the highlights that struck Frank so forcefully the first time he saw her.

In April of 1923, Rissie began to fear the worst and she could see the toll it was taking on her brother. On the last day of the month, the family gathered in the living room of Frank and Manie Ethel's house in the camps to support her in what was becoming her last fight. The camp doctor had tried his best, and all the healers of the creek had tried as well, but pneumonia had set in, and the end was near. As she failed, Frank's younger brother Jesse was dispatched to bring the doctor, but by the time he arrived, Manie Ethel Hopkins was already gone.

Rissie said Frank was on his knees beside the bed when she took her last breath and had stopped breathing himself, as if he were afraid he would steal the very air from his dying wife. When her chest heaved no more, he fell across it, and yielded to his brain screaming for oxygen that she could no longer take in. She said his moan sounded like a drowning man, gasping for the air that had been denied him for almost too long. Then he began to wail as only a solider would, after looking down at his body and seeing arms or legs missing and his life's blood pouring out on the ground. Rissie knew that was what was happening to Frank; his heart was emptying itself forever on the lifeless body of the only woman he had ever loved.

Rissie walked upstairs, where Frank's only living child, in fever and pain, was sleeping fitfully in the bedroom above his mother's death chamber. She lifted him from his crib, clutched him to her, and sat down in a rocking chair.

I will not lose you, she thought, not like I gave up the others. Nothing will ever hurt you again, as long as there is a breath in me. Nothing in this world. Nothing in any world.

The child began to calm, and when she felt his breath become steady, only then did she allow herself to weep for Manie Ethel Hopkins.

*   *   *

In September of 1923, the McKinney Steel Company, as part of its plan to make its Kentucky coal operations the most modern and technologically advanced in the nation, furnished its miners with hard hats and electric lamps. Few other mines had them, and in fact most companies would not even furnish calcium carbide for their employees' lamps, which they also had to supply for themselves. Young Jesse Hopkins, through Frank's recommendation, got the job of lamp boy, and worked nights charging the batteries the miners picked up every morning.

The Company issued new hard hats and electric lamps to the men in September 1923. All were happy to receive the new gear and smiled broadly for the photographer. Frank Hopkins is in the front row, third from the left.

The company brought Frank's section crew out of the mine for a photograph for a newspaper article. To keep coal moving, the men were brought out five or six at a time and the different pictures were cut and pasted into one composite. The men were each given a copy of the final picture and Frank's was still in the trunk we opened in 1977. He is kneeling in the front row and is the only man not grinning broadly at this latest innovation by McKinney Steel. He is not even smiling; at the time, Manie Ethel had not been long in her grave and it seemed his last son, Marvin, would soon join his mother and brother.

But Rissie would not accept that. Frank had made no protest when she took charge after Frank came back to his father's house with his possessions. Since he no longer had a family, he did not need to pay rent on a camp house. Frank left Harrison's house in the morning for his job and came back every evening, after stopping by the Old Prater Cemetery, and let Rissie tend to the child. He thought it was only a matter of time before Marvin succumbed as well.

Rissie, of course, would never accept that. She took him to her sister Alice when he needed breast milk and stayed with him all night when Manie Ethel's parents wanted him. She took him regularly to the camp doctor and consulted with all the old wives on Greasy Creek, using every resource she had to get him to sleep, to eat and to gain weight. Frank permitted her to take care of him, but did not think Marvin would live. He planned to let Paris and Nina take the child; he worried the responsibility of tending a dying child would be too much for Rissie to deal with when Marvin's time came.

In 1925, Paris Coleman had two brothers left after his brother Lon and most of his family died of typhoid the previous year. One brother, Melvin, and his wife Virginia, taught school together until Melvin decided to go into farming to supply camp residents with vegetables and the occasional "medicine" needed for a hot toddy to fight off a chill. He quietly built a still on his property and Virginia delivered the product to those housewives who needed it, for medicinal purposes only. She drove a two-wheeled cart, propelled by an elderly horse that plodded obediently from house to house as she made her rounds.

The other brother, Ernest, had a son who began school in Virginia's classroom, but would not do his lessons. After several attempts to make him work, she sent him home to his father. The next day, the youth returned "with a brace of pistols," according to the *Pike County News*. Virginia sent for the school trustee, who promptly expelled the boy. Ernest tried to get his son back in school, but Virginia and the school trustee refused. When neither the Upper or Lower Greasy Grade Schools, nor the camp school allowed him entrance, Ernest began spreading rumors about Virginia, hoping to get her replaced by someone more amenable. Virginia took him to court for slander.

Virginia was not successful, largely because the word of a woman against a man was not worth much in that era. On the way back from Pikeville, where both had gone only to see the case dismissed, Ernest harassed Virginia continually about her loss. When they got off the train, Ernest followed Virginia through the town, laughing and shouting until she pulled out a revolver and shot her tormentor.

He was not badly wounded, and spent only a night in the hospital, but when he was released he found the tables had turned. She had not been arrested and had not lost her job. The authorities considered her actions self-defense, and Ernest was now the object of ridicule. "Hey, Ern," men teased him. "I hear you got shot by a woman." It was one of the most humiliating insults a man could receive.

Ernest, who already had a drinking problem, retreated further into the bottle in anger, and began to drink most of the day. He was warned by his bosses his job was in jeopardy for his drinking and increasing failure to show up for work. He often came out on his porch to stare as Virginia passed with her horse and cart. Before long, he was observed to be carrying a pistol and once shot up into the air to frighten her. Finally, in his stupor, he shot the old horse in the flank, the bullet whistling by Virginia's face. She pulled out the same pistol she'd shot him with earlier and fired while attempting to restrain the wounded animal. When she calmed the horse and looked back, Ernest was lying in a pool of blood on his front porch. Her bullet had hit him directly in the heart.

In the turmoil that followed, Paris did not want to take either brother's side and announced to Frank that he planned to take his family to Ohio and they would take the child with them. Rissie became nearly hysterical; she had saved Marvin's life and she would not let anyone take him away from her. Frank, finally able to see through the grief that had overpowered him, realized that Rissie was the only one who would not give up on his son.

"If he dies," he told his father-in-law. "I'll let him die here." The Colemans moved away and Marvin stayed with Rissie. He did not die and Rissie became the wise and caring mother no one had thought she would ever be. Years later, when Frank married again and came for his boy, she would not give him up.

"No," she said. "You gave him to me and he's mine. If you want to keep him some you can, but you know Laura wants her own children. She won't want Manie's child. She won't love him like I do and you know that, Frank Hopkins."

Rissie's argument made sense; he could not deny the wisdom in her logic and he walked away. The stage was set for my siblings and me to grow up with three grandparents. We never thought it unusual, and indeed it was not; other families were often mixed with orphans. With all

Rissie and Marvin, 1924

the death and loss in the coal fields at the time of my father's birth, with all the husbands and fathers killed by roof falls and explosions, and with all the sickness and disease, our situation was not that atypical.

*　　　*　　　*

For fifty years, the Hebrews were in exile, until the Persians rescued them from the Babylonians. For half a century their homeland was lost, yet they survived because their god told them that someday they would return. In the 1920's in the coal fields, my people were also in bondage, but they sought no return to the past. Unlike the Hebrews, they did not resist their enslavement and adopted the faith of their captors. They erected no shrines to the new gods, but flocked to worship with each payday. They were in thrall to this prosperous new life in which everything they wanted was now within reach. They never knew how deep was their captivity.

On Thursday, February 23, 1928, the *Pike County News* published its regular edition which was brought to Greasy Creek on the morning train. People in the camp eagerly awaited the paper and looked for their names and news of the camp under "Greasy Creek" in the society section. The first entry was usually about the camp bosses:

Our superintendent, Mr. Dean, has been in hospital for a few days. We hope he will soon be feeling well again.

In another paragraph, a family named Good took some special pride:

Miss Ruth Evelyn Good is given up to be the prettiest baby on Greasy Creek and that's that!

Price McKinney, were he still alive, would have been proud to see the progress the town had made on his progressive social agenda:

The Junior Order of United American Mechanics met and organized here Saturday night. There was a good crowd and everything went off smoothly.

The First Aid work is going over the top on Greasy Creek. Mr. Preston, Mr. Dean, Mr. Crane and others are pushing this phase of mining.

Dr. Butterworth is mighty busy inoculating everybody here for typhoid since the death of Mrs. Coleman. Safety first always, here with the authorities.

A word of guidance to the young was found in these lines:

Uncle Wess McCown, nearly 80 years old, works six days a week at hard labor. If the young men were this busy, there wouldn't be so many idle minds to supply the devil with workshops.

The article had no byline, but it was a regular column that continued in the paper for another fifty years. The author may have not lived on Greasy Creek, but he or she knew well the mood of the people who lived in the camp:

Greasy Creek mines are working five days a week. The company houses are nearly all full, and the miners are well satisfied because they get a fair deal. It seems that most people who leave Greasy Creek want to come back, as they feel it's home.

The paragraph was ample evidence, if anyone needed it, of the regard the miners had for the company and the town Price McKinney had built. It was more than mere gratitude for a job; there was true loyalty and affection among the men. A new chapter had been written in Greasy Creek history, and even those who could not read put aside their copies of the paper for safekeeping.

The following week, the column did not run. The editor had too many corrections to make and decided not to publish. He was not sure when, or if, he would run the column again. The Corrigan-McKinney Steel Company had closed the Greasy Creek mine forever.

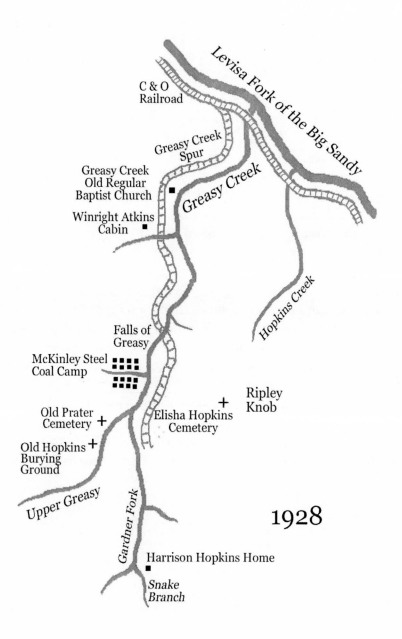

Greasy Creek
Camp, 1928.
Looking west.

Greasy Creek Camp, 1928. Looking up Big Bug Hollow, where
the houses of the Big Bugs (company executives) were located.
Although most coal camp houses were painted uniformly white,
Price McKinney ordered the houses of Greasy Creek painted in
alternating colors to eliminate monotony and provide a more
pleasant environment for the families living there. Of all the
houses in this picture, only the large structure in the center, the
Greasy Creek Hotel, still stands.

Snow

*R*issie was worried. She had been uneasy before they came to the party and now her nervousness was showing. She saw disaster waiting for her through every window in the room. She had tasted snow in the air when she left her father's house with Harlen earlier that evening and now it was beginning. It was New Year's Eve, and she hoped it would hold off until midnight, when the party would be over, and they could have made it back up the old Gardner Fork road with no difficulty, but now the streets of the town were covered. It was barely eleven and she could the snow coming down steadily. The big clock behind the now-unused front desk of the hotel seemed to slow its agonizing pace and stop moving altogether.

This will be awful, she thought. What did I get myself into? If I have to walk in the snow, I'll fall and make a fool of myself. He'll be ashamed of me. I told him it would snow and I couldn't go, but he insisted. I shouldn't have come.

I shouldn't have come. I shouldn't have come.

She had to admit this was mostly her fault. Harlen was playing music; she didn't want to miss any opportunity to be with him, and this was special. The caretaker of the hotel had allowed Harlen and his boys to play there, in spite of the fact that it was closed, with no maids and no one working in the kitchen.

The company, or at least the caretaker, had allowed the use of the hotel as if the camps were still running and there was some reason to celebrate, but no coal had moved off Greasy Creek for the better part of a year, and people were beginning to worry. Some began to doubt that the mine would ever come back to life. There were precious few company jobs now; the caretaker had one of them, and his duties were mostly to look after the darkened buildings where men used to come and go in droves: offices, shops, even the now-closed hospital. Rissie wondered if one of his jobs was to keep up the spirits of the remaining residents, so that the men would be there when the whistle blew again, and if that was why he agreed to let Harlen and the boys have a dance.

Harlen could play anything anyone wanted to hear on his banjo, and the crowd was happy, even though the cost of admission, ten cents a person and fifteen cents a couple, was harder to come by this year, especially with Christmas just a week ago. Still, the boys had made a little money, and Rissie knew that she could not leave until the new year came; that much was owed those who had paid to get in.

Although the great mine was idle, there were many other places where men could find work and most of them had gone, at least the men who were not born on Greasy Creek. Only a few of the Greasy Creek boys had pulled up stakes however; many did not live in company houses and did not have to pay rent. They waited in their homes until they were called back. More truthfully, the men who remained did so for a different reason: if they got killed, and the odds were they would, they wanted to be close to home, where they could be put away without the additional expense of shipping their crushed bodies back from whatever alien camp they had migrated.

Some of the boys had moved to Virginia and West Virginia and were gone over Christmas. John and Bessie were still living in Buchanan County, but had come home to stay with Harrison, where Bessie's children could play with Marvin. Bessie loved Marvin almost as much as Rissie did, but then all Harrison's children loved the boy Rissie had saved.

"Go ahead with Harlen," Bessie told Rissie earlier that day. "You go have you a good time, Sissy, you never go anywhere. I'll take care of the baby."

Why didn't I stay with them, Rissie asked herself, now that they're all safe in bed? I'm down here in the camps and it's snowing and I'll never get home with this foot.

She felt guilty if she left Marvin for anything.

The snow's piling up, she thought, and he'll think I'm not coming home. She had a brief moment of panic and started to get her coat to begin the treacherous walk alone, but when Harlen looked at her while he was singing, she knew she could not leave until the last chord had been plucked on his banjo.

He is so beautiful, she thought, what does he see in me? Look at him; look at those strong arms, those beautiful teeth. There's so many pretty girls here; he could have any of them he wants. I can't even dance to his music. What does he want with me?

She made the decision to stay in spite of her misgivings and now it was too late to change her mind. The great company clock seemed to move again, more rapidly than before, and now sped dizzily toward midnight. Rissie realized that she had waited too long and now the roads would be slick, too slick for her to walk with any semblance of grace. Her greatest fear would soon be realized and Harlen would see her for the cripple she was. When the clock struck twelve the party would be over and everyone would leave and she would not be able to hide it: she would fall and Harlen would be ashamed of her and regret he had spent New Year's Eve with her and she would never see him again.

Then the chimes began, counting out the last minutes of 1928, and Rissie's heart jumped into her throat. As the clock struck twelve, the cries went up in the room, and she could see kisses stolen in every part of it. Almost as if she were in a dream or in a picture show with a failing projector, the guests began to leave, until only the band remained with their girl-

friends. Rissie walked toward them. Harlen was dividing up the money they had made and the two other boys left, jangling the coins in their pockets. Their girlfriends were smiling.

"Well, Rissie, we had us a good night," Harlen said. "Did you enjoy yourself?"

"Yes, but I told you it was going to snow," she replied. *Could he see how much this bothered her? If he did, he did not show it. He paid the company caretaker, EB Mullins, who had been the payroll clerk for the mine before it closed.* "You be careful out there," *he told Rissie, and began turning out the lights. If the camps were still running these lights would be on all the time, Rissie thought and big shots would have been here, and everyone would be laughing and having a good time.*

But if the camps were still running, she thought, we wouldn't be here anyway.

"Ah, a little snow never hurt nobody," Harlen said, *as he took down his coat from the pegs near the door, along with Rissie's, and held hers out.* "Bundle up here, girl. It might be cold outside."

Rissie wrapped her scarf around her and put her hands into her muff. It had belonged to her mother, and she had been as proud of it as Rissie was when her father gave it to her. It was one of the few luxuries the Hopkins family had. They walked out onto the porch and into the flat street. The snow was already ankle-deep; now she was truly frightened. Walking through the camps would be no problem, but the road up Gardner was neither flat nor straight.

She had no choice; she had to head off disaster.

"Harlen," she said. "I don't think I can make it home in this snow, and it's still coming down. If you can help me get to Uncle Harmon's, I'll just stay there, and you can go on up Gardner and tell Daddy where I am."

"All right," he said. *In the near darkness, she thought she could see him smile; in fact, he seemed actually to be grinning.*

It was strange to see all the houses with no lights, no one living in them, and there was no one but the departing crowd left on the street. What will we do if the mine don't open back up, she wondered?

As they left the street and followed the dirt road up to the forks of Greasy Creek, just above the camps, Rissie could sense her footing begin to slip. She walked carefully and Harlen walked deliberately beside her, never offering a clue that he wanted to move faster. They talked about the dance, about the prospects for work when the mine and the town came back and shared gossip they had heard. Then for the first time, Rissie noticed that Harlen did not have his banjo case with him.

"Harlen, did you forget your banjo?" she asked breath-lessly. "We'd better go back and get it."

"No," he said. "I sent it home with the boys."

That was unusual, she thought; Harlen would never let anyone handle his banjo but him. He watched over it like a hawk, and he lets it go on New Year's Eve?

They took the left fork and walked toward Harmon Robin-son's big two-story house. The lights were still on and she felt relieved that she would have a place to stay. She could also see further on that Aunt Malissy's lights still glowed. She could stay there too, but what she wanted mostly was to get back to her boy. When she started to turn in at Harmon's gate, Harlen nudged her forward.

"Harlen, I got to go in here," she said in protest.

"No, you don't," he replied.

She was on the verge of tears; she could not walk the rest of the way to her father's house. She would fall and he would have to pick her up. She would be humiliated. Don't he understand that?

"Harlen, I can't walk up this road with this foot," she said finally. "You know I can't."

"You can't?" he asked in mock incredulity. "Well, then I'll just have to carry you."

With those words, he bent down and effortlessly scooped her up. Even through the thicknesses of his coat and hers, she could feel the power of the muscles in his arms and chest. She felt as if the wind had picked her up and dropped her in his arms.

"Harlen, put me down," she said in protest. "You can't carry me all the way to Daddy's."

"Well, if I can't, then we'll just take a break every now and then."

Rissie suddenly realized that this was not something he had done on impulse. He had planned it all the time; he knew it would snow and this would give him the excuse he needed to hold her. She did not protest as his lips met hers.

"Put me down now," she said softly, as the kiss was broken. How long had he held her? She wasn't sure. She

Harlen Damron. When Harlan asked Rissie what she wanted for her 36th birthday, she told him she wanted a real portrait of him, taken by a professional. The Pikeville photographer supplied the jacket and tie he wore. The photograph remained on her mantle until she died in 1977. It was the same photograph she used for his tombstone and it has never faded.

wasn't sure even where she was. He took her hand and they stared in the semi-darkness into each other's eyes. It was no longer winter to Rissie; it may have just been her flushed face, but it felt warm, like June, and if the clouds passed, she would not have been surprised to see fireflies instead of stars. When her heart quit pounding, she turned up the old Gardner Fork road toward her house.

Twice more, as the road became perilous, Harlen picked her up and carried her past the danger. Twice more they kissed, and twice more her heart nearly jumped out of her chest. By the time they arrived at Harrison's house, the snow was a foot deep. Before they went inside, she looked back at the snowflakes and remembered what her grandmother had told her about a wedding that was planned on a night much like this, when the snow fell on two cousins who had just walked off Ripley Knob after one of them had said good-bye to her beloved.

She had only three days as a wife, Rissie thought, but she was happy. If that's all I could have, I'd take it, too.

"I love you, Rissie," he said. "I always have. I want you to marry me."

She could not believe her ears. Had she fallen in the snow and was unconscious, dreaming this?

When she found her voice, she could only say, "I've got the boy, Harlen. I've got Marvin. If you want me, you have to want him too. He has to be your boy, too."

"Rissie, I swear..." Harlen stumbled in his reply. "I promise you I want him too. I always have. I want him to be my boy. I want you both. I'll take care of both of you as long as I live."

Rissie looked at his face. She could see that he was fearful she would not believe him. She shook her head no, but only to say to herself that she did believe him, that she knew he was truthful, but then realized he would misinterpret what she was doing. She became motionless and looked up at him.

"All right," she said. "I will."

She was sure she could feel his heart beating as he pulled her close, if it wasn't her own, or if it wasn't both of them beating together.

Her family was waiting for them when they came in out of the cold.

A Killing Frost

Some yet consult the *Old Farmer's Almanac* to see if the "signs" are right for farming on Greasy Creek. They know there are certain crops that will wilt or leaf out profusely without bearing fruit, if the signs are in the bowels or the heart when the seeds are planted. Some are even more prescient and have a gift for judging the weather. They know when it is too early to plant, even if the signs are right, or when they should take in the last of the summer's bounty before it is lost. I do not know if that is an art that can be learned or if it is passed down through the genes of natural farmers, but I wonder if, some eighty years ago, anyone could have read something in the wind or stars.

There was no warning when the mine closed. No production schedules had been changed. No rumors were spread, and no knowing glances exchanged between supervisors. No orders for supplies had been cancelled or even reduced. The employment office had continued to interview applicants and company management asked my great-grandfather Luke Hamlin, who operated a general merchandise store on the edge of camp, if he would consider running the new commissary when it was built. He said he would think about it.

Engineers put the finishing touches on the survey for the new camp, between the times they adjusted the underground maps as the shafts penetrated farther and farther into the mountain Ripley Knob commanded. Anemometer readings were taken, brattice curtains adjusted and ventilation fans added to pull more air to the face of the seam where miners good-naturedly harassed their chums in the martial camaraderie of men who face the possibility of death together every day.

Trains came and went, and the 3:00 p.m. shuttle to Pikeville picked up and disgorged passengers regularly. Miners' wives washed clothes and hung them out to dry on porches and lines strung between houses as they always did, fed their children sturdy breakfasts before sending them off to school, and then sauntered over to neighbor's porches to exchange gossip.

If anyone on Greasy Creek knew something was afoot, it would have been IB Sanders, who respected the signs but had a closer connection to the company. He had hosted Price McKinney in his home and had worried about the future since he heard of what happened in Cleveland in 1925. He would not have been surprised three years later, when that worry came to fruition.

In truth, however, the seed for the destruction of the Greasy Creek camp was planted on the day in 1917 that McKinney changed the name of the company. It enraged Jimmy Corrigan when he heard of it, but he could do nothing for seven years, until he reached forty and his majority as his father had determined it. For a year after receiving control of his shares, he bedeviled Price McKinney, who continued to ignore him until he had enough and made plans to remove his nemesis from the board of McKinney Steel.

Jimmy Corrigan heard of the plans, and with his wife's assistance, raised a down payment of five million dollars to purchase enough stock from the late Judge Burke's heirs to amass another 13% of the company. Added to his own 40%, he now had enough stock to do the unthinkable and oust Price McKinney from the company he had spent thirty years building up to the tenth-largest (and one of the most profitable) steel-making businesses in America.

It would be difficult to imagine the shock and humiliation McKinney would have suffered when Jimmy Corrigan walked into the boardroom with Judge Burke's proxy and sent him packing. Perhaps only the miners on Greasy Creek, three years later, could have experienced anything so devastating. McKinney now had no function, no voice in company decisions, and no way to ensure that his workers would be treated fairly. Although a millionaire, he was now out of a job, out of the only job he truly ever loved, out of the company that bore his name. Jimmy Corrigan did not remove McKinney's name completely (it was now known as the *Corrigan-McKinney* Steel Company), but he made it clear that Price McKinney would never again be part of it.

One day, without giving anyone a hint of his disposition, and with his horses at Wycliffe grazing contentedly on new spring grass, McKinney went into his study and picked up a memento of the Great War and stared at it. It was a Luger taken from a surrendered officer of the defeated German Army. It had been given to McKinney by a friend in the US Army as a token of appreciation for the service he and McKinney Steel had rendered to the war effort on the home front.

He put the weapon to his head and pulled the trigger. The date was April 13, 1926, some eight months after McKinney lost control of his company.

In spite of the hard glances of McKinney's family, a shocked Jimmy Corrigan followed the funeral procession to Lake View Cemetery, where McKinney was interred just a few steps from Captain Jim. He was alone in the limousine; Laura Mae had left her London mansion for France and she rarely came to America anyway. She always went to Paris to take spring; there was simply no other place to be in April.

But April was pretty in Cleveland that year, especially in Lake View Cemetery, where Price McKinney was laid to rest close to his best friend, in the plots he had purchased for both of them. Jimmy wondered if his father could have anticipated that his son would become his best friend's worst enemy. That may have been part of the strain of attempting to run a great corporation for which he had no training, but after McKinney's death, he found himself more and more returning to the practices that his predecessor had proven so successful. The plans he had approved for Greasy Creek were continued and, except for replacing the signs on company property, the Corrigan-McKinney Steel Company did not change much at all.

In January 1928, Jimmy Corrigan was dreading another sea voyage. He did not like the water; he had memories of his family drowning far from shore. The *Titanic* had proven that nothing was unsinkable, but he could put Laura Mae off no longer. She had insisted he come to France this year and he had been busy making plans for the company to run for a few months without him. After a busy morning, he had developed a terrific head-ache, and decided to visit the Cleveland Athletic Club to relax and have lunch.

Halfway through the front door, he staggered and fell dead of an aneurysm. The company cabled Laura Mae, who booked passage on the first ship home. Jimmy's body was kept in cold storage until she arrived.

Not long after the funeral, Laura Mae Whitlock McMartin Corrigan walked into the offices of the Union Trust Company to inquire of her finances. She would not be staying long in Cleveland and in fact had already booked passage for England, but she had some issues to settle first. Her husband had left her his share of the company under much the same arrangement that his father had set up for him: she could benefit from her shares, but she could not vote them. Union Trust would make all decisions for her and she could go back to Europe and not worry. She would receive a monthly support check in addition to her regular dividends, but she was concerned with maintaining her standard of living. The company said she would receive $10,000 monthly, independent of her dividends, but that was just not enough. Although her husband had been generous and she had other investments, she needed more money. She wanted to sell her share of the company.

The problem was that Union Trust had told her the company was not worth $100 million as she thought; it was appraised at

$65 million because of indebtedness caused by recent expansion plans. In the Kentucky coal operations, one camp was not yet complete, although coal was flowing from the mine. It would be two years before the expansion was finished and the company recovered its investment. Her fifty-three percent was suddenly worth much less than she expected.

Laura Mae knew assets and she knew the more profitable a company was, the higher sale price it would command. She may have surprised the accountants with her awareness of such a basic business premise; certainly she would have surprised them with the force of her personality, but they were stunned when she demanded a review of the company balance sheet. She gave them two days to prepare the report.

"Why are we spending more money on this place, Greasy Creek?" she asked, possibly with a hint of distaste as she pronounced the words. "What is this money set aside for?" She pointed to an entry in the ledger. "It seems excessive."

"It is for the third camp," one of the accountants spoke up. "We intend to build a hundred more houses so that we will have an equivalency between Wolfpit and Greasy Creek."

"You plan to double the number of employees on Greasy Creek?" Laura inquired, raising one finely groomed eyebrow. "Why is that? Do we not have a sufficient supply of coal with our current operations?"

"Yes we do, either mine can supply our current needs," the accountant said. "But we will inevitably expand and need more coal. Even should we not, Mr. Corrigan wanted to ensure that we would have no interruptions in the supply in the event one of the mines were to close for any reason."

"But we have sufficient coal with only one operation, yes?"

"Yes, Ma'am, but..."

"And Wolfpit is the larger operation?"

"Yes, Ma'am, but..."

"And Greasy Creek is yet incomplete?"

"Yes, Ma'am, but Mr. Corrigan's business plan was to have a redundancy..."

"I should remind you," Laura Mae said, adopting her most winsome look. "That Mr. Corrigan has passed away."

"Yes, Ma'am, and you have our deepest sympathies, but Mr. Corrigan was implementing the successful plan of Mr. McKinney, who..."

"I should also remind you," she interrupted. "That Mr. McKinney is gone as well."

Before long, the accountants would have concluded that they had met their match. After she left, all the proposed expenditures for the Greasy Creek camp were erased. Her yearly stipend was increased to $142,500 until her shares, estimated at $30 million, were sold. With an improved balance sheet, she thought, they should fetch another five million dollars.

A single-sentence paragraph appeared in the March 2, 1928 edition of the *Pike County News*: "The Corrigan-McKinney Steel Company has announced it is closing the Greasy Creek mine to concentrate on its operations at Wolfpit."

No other information was given and the company managers would say nothing about the move, mostly because they were as bewildered as the workers. The message had been telegraphed to Greasy Creek from Cleveland with instructions to close the mine immediately and transfer all the men to the Wolfpit operations. Those who wished to live in company houses on Greasy Creek could continue for a period of time if they worked at Wolfpit, but many decided to take jobs somewhere else. Jobs were plentiful in the coal fields, and the shockwave that rolled through Greasy Creek dissolved in a heartbeat most of the loyalty the men once felt for the company.

By then, Laura Mae was back in London and had donned her finely tailored widow's reeds to accept the condolences and sympathy of her fellow London socialites. After a week of receiving, she advised her secretary to express her regrets, but she had departed for Paris to recuperate. She had not fully recovered from learning her share of the company was worth so little, but that would soon be corrected. If she had to tighten her belt, so would Corrigan-McKinney Steel. The mathematics of her expectations were easy to understand, and the company Price McKinney saved from extinction and built up to one of the most progressive and profitable steel companies in America now had a "For Sale" sign in its window.

*   *   *

For a time, it was difficult for me to reconcile the opposing stories I heard of what it was like to mine coal in the old days. On one hand, I had the testaments of those who had worked in the Greasy Creek mine and fondly remembered what it was like to receive a good day's pay for a good day's work. On the other hand, I heard stories of men who would come home long after dark, so blackened with coal dust that they would pass no farther into their homes than the kitchen, where they would take a meal and stretch out behind the stove to sleep for a few hours until they went back to work. They would pass to and from the mines in darkness, never seeing daylight or their children.

My problem in sorting out the contradiction was that I was too immersed in the American concept of success, since my father had a good job at the Republic Steel Company mine not far from Greasy Creek. He had a modern bathhouse at work, just like the men had on Greasy Creek decades before. He had a union contract, good health and retirement benefits for both him and my mother, and he made enough money to help his three children go to college. I was a Baby Boomer; I had been taught directly and indirectly that the story of America is the story of success, of increase, of regular elevation of the standard of living and continual improvement in working conditions for laborers from year to year.

So to make sense of the conflicting stories, I concluded that when men spoke of working like dogs only a day or two a week, they were talking of some Dark Age in the coal industry that existed *before* Price McKinney came to Greasy Creek. But the men who complained of the wretched conditions they endured were largely *younger* than the men who worked in the McKinney Steel mine.

What I did not know was that although there were two eras, I had them reversed: the hard times came *after* the Greasy Creek mine was closed.

It did not happen immediately; for a year and a half, the rest of Pike County boomed along with the whole country as companies and their workers made and spent money wildly. Installment credit flourished and postmen strained under the load of mail order catalogs. Banks lent money easily, in spite of the fact that savings accounts, from which they were supposed to lend money with good stewardship, diminished as people eschewed savings for consumer goods. Banks began borrowing from other banks to lend more money. Common stock of large corporations supplied much of the collateral for certain borrowers who, even in Pike County, used the proceeds of their loans to buy more stock. Although Greasy Creek had few stockholders in any company, the economy continued to surge, as men simply walked across the mountains to Marrowbone Creek or Little Creek where jobs awaited them.

On a national level, however, the economy was dangerously overheated. Debt increased on private, public, and corporate levels. Stock issues were snapped up as soon as they were released, often by people who had never bought paper of any kind and who would not have attended a stockholders meeting if they knew what it was or where it was being held.

And then, like a child's house of cards, it all tumbled.

There had been blips; occasionally a news article would relate the story of a bank that had closed somewhere or, due to temporary overstock of inventory, a particular plant would take an extended holiday. But on the same page would be stories about some new product creating a whole new industry. Not until the stock market fell precipitously, then recovered, then crashed resoundingly, did the faltering economy slide into catastrophe.

Almost overnight, there were far too many people in the coal fields for the work that was available. Wages were cut almost as soon as the stock market collapsed and cut again and again as the Depression deepened. It would have been worse had the First World War not cut off the flow of immigrants from Europe in 1914. Now, instead of sending emissaries to distant coal fields or neighboring camps to find labor to work the mines, the companies suddenly found themselves with a surfeit of men desperate for work. They also found they could pay the men a fraction of what they once paid and the workers would be grateful just to have a job.

By 1938, the US Census bureau reported the average annual wage for a bituminous coal miner was $525. It took five more years and another world war for American miners to average over a thousand dollars in a single year. But even those figures are deceiving; many miners had no homes for the census takers to enumerate and hordes of men out of work had left their families to fend with relatives or friends. If a man wanted to work, he had to take whatever he could get. The stories of exhausted, dirty men sleeping on kitchen floors were not hyperbole.

In 1930, in reaction to the slumping economy and declining orders for steel, Corrigan-McKinney could no longer justify keeping a skeleton crew on Greasy Creek to keep the power plant running, maintain the pumps in the mine, or paint the company buildings. The shafts began to fill with water, and sections of the roof, propped by crumbling timbers that yielded to wet or dry rot, began to fall. The unfinished commissary stood in mute testimony to the town's reversal of fortune, as what would have been a vast concrete basement was now a pond, as the structure filled with rainwater, engendering generations of frogs and snakes that lived there for fifty years.

About the same time, the railroads began to feel the pinch of reduced traffic and cut their rates. Their largest competitors for freight had been the steamboats, whose largest customers had been the railroads as coal camps were being built, off-loading lumber and roofing in vast quantities at makeshift towns up and down the Big Sandy. The rate reductions were the last straw for the boat owners. They had sponsored numerous efforts to have the Kentucky General Assembly lock and dam the river, but the railroad interests blatantly bought off the elected representatives of the state. When the Depression came, there was too little money for such projects anyway, and the owners, who could no longer afford to dredge the sandbars and pull snags with their own money, finally gave up.

The young boys who waited on the Pikeville bridge with pockets full of corncobs no longer had targets for their childish villainy. The boats had gone and would never return. There was no fanfare when the last one left and no one is certain of when it was or even its name, but the time of the riverboats on the Big Sandy, the glorious era that began in 1837 and lasted almost a century, ended without a eulogy.

Also in 1930, the Union Trust Company cabled Laura Mae they were having trouble finding a buyer because of the declines in the national economy, but it was certain the slump would not last. However, it would be unlikely her stock would bring the price it would have two years before. She was dumfounded; her plan was not going well. The estimated value of her stock had dropped to only $22 million. She cabled them back and said she would be in Cleveland within the month.

Laura Mae Whitlock McMartin Corrigan knew when to cut her losses. She lifted her siege of Cleveland early on, when no one returned her invitations, and shifted her efforts to New York. Although she had a sponsor in a wizened Astor whose finances no longer allowed her the exclusivity she once could demand, Laura Mae knew early on how successful she would be in America. When the return on her New York investment would not justify the cost, she pulled out and went to the continent. She had a gambler's sense of when to fold, and even though she would not get what she deserved from Corrigan-McKinney, she again recognized the moment.

She would sell her shares now.

* * *

On a warm late April Sunday afternoon on Greasy Creek, Rissie walked down the mountain from her cabin on Ripley Knob to visit Malissa Prater. As usual, she had Marvin in tow, and wanted Aunt Malissy to see how he had grown. It was 1931 and Marvin was soon to be nine years old; she was proud of her boy.

In front of Malissa's house, IB Sanders's car was parked. *I heard that IB had quit driving and had his boys do it, she thought. He must be 75 at least.*

She could see IB sitting on Malissa's porch with her, along with three other women, one of whom she recognized. She thought she remembered younger versions of the other two. It had been almost ten years since she saw Mary Jane Willoughby and the other two were her daughters.

"Rissie," Malissa asked loudly, for either Mary Jane or IB to hear. "You remember Mrs. Willoughby, don't you?"

"Yes, Ma'am," Rissie replied. "I thought it was you. How are you Miss Willoughby? I'm so sorry I couldn't come to Asa or Grafton's funerals."

"Don't you worry, darlin'," Mary Jane said. "Aunt Malissy told me about your troubles. Is this your boy?"

Marvin peeked out from behind his mother's dress. "Yes, Ma'am. He'll be nine this year."

"He's a good-lookin' boy," Mary Jane said, looking at him almost mournfully. "He'll make a fine man one of these days."

"Did you come up to see your Daddy's grave?" Rissie asked. "We've been tryin' to keep it up."

"Partly," Mary Jane said cryptically. "I want to thank you and Aunt Malissy for taking care of it. She said you and her decorate it just like your own."

"Yes, Ma'am. We all thought a lot of your daddy."

"Mary Jane just lost Jesse," Malissa gently interrupted. "It was a roof fall down at that mine he was workin' in Floyd County."

Rissie was shocked; her face fell and her eyes misted. *Bless her heart, Rissie thought. Now she's lost both her boys and her man. No wonder she looks so hurt.* Rissie embraced the older woman.

"I'm so sorry, Miss Willoughby. If there's anything I can do for you, just let me know."

Mary Jane reached down to caress Marvin's hair as he looked confusedly at the woman who was clutching his mother. "There is," she said. "You can keep him out of the mines, any way you can."

Rissie sat down with the women and talked as Marvin played under Malissa's porch. After a while, IB gently announced it was time to go to Pikeville to catch the evening train. It would be a long ride to Muhlenberg County and Rissie knew the trip would be hard on her. Rissie looked to the cemetery on the hill above Malissa's house. William Bracken was buried there, near where her mother was buried, where the Hopkinses and the Praters rested and she felt a chill in spite of the warm day. *Another April, Rissie thought. Why do things always happen just when the hills are coming to life again?*

"I don't know when I'll be back," Mary Jane said as they stepped off the porch. "I really appreciate you taking care of Dad's grave." Malissa and Rissie promised her they would and they both sensed that this would be the last time Mary Jane would ever see Greasy Creek.

The women waved to each other a last time as IB's car pulled across the creek onto the road and aimed for the deserted town. Rissie wondered if IB felt compelled to drive the women since he had brought Grafton to Greasy Creek. *At least her boys didn't die here, or Grafton either, she thought. IB won't have to grieve over that. Mary Jane's daddy was just old; it was his time.*

As the car disappeared down the empty street, she wondered, for the hundredth or two hundredth time, if the Greasy Creek mine would ever reopen. She wasn't sure she wanted that to happen all that much; then the boys would just begin dying again. That came with coal mining, but men had to work; they had to feed their families. She felt the chill again, as if she knew the final toll of the mine had yet to be collected.

*   *   *

The first house Rissie and Harlen moved into with their son was a small cabin perched on a flat above the store and nearby home of Big Will Hopkins, just up Gardner Fork from Harmon Robinson's house. The store building had been constructed long before the mine came by Thomas Jefferson Robinson, Harmon's oldest son. It had been dismantled and brought to its current site when the McKinney Steel Company bought TJ out. The Robinsons continued to operate it when the mine was running, but it closed when the Depression came along.

Big Will decided to buy it from TJ after Martha Ellen, Will's wife and TJ's cousin, encouraged him to quit walking all the way to Wolfpit to work when his job trickled down to only a day or two a week. Will had been transferred to Wolfpit when Greasy Creek closed, but work was so slow he decided to take his chances operating a store. Will was an honest man and was fair to his customers. Times were hard, but he extended as much credit as he could and most of his customers paid their bills. Will made enough money for his family to live on and let Rissie and Harlen live rent-free above them.

Martha Ellen was Harlen's older sister and just above them lived their father Jack Damron. His cabin was on the same flat where Elisha's cabin had stood until its ruins burned to the ground years before. Blackberry vines and a wild tangle of bushes and roses nearly covered the site, but Rissie still visited the cemetery and cut pale, pink roses, nearly white, from the copse that spread protectively across the blackened bones of the ancient structure.

Rissie would have been proud to live in the cabin had it still existed, but Harlen built her a small house that was perfect for the new couple, although Rissie would have liked to have a larger garden and a cow. Marvin was growing like a weed and he needed milk, so she walked up Gardner every evening to milk the cow Harrison kept. She had moved out from Harrison's when she and Harlen got married and her brother Jesse moved in with Pearl, his new wife. All the rest of Harrison's children had married and moved away.

Harrison would sometimes climb the path up to Rissie's house to spend the night with her when Jesse and Pearl had arguments, which were becoming more frequent. Jesse seemed unable to accept that his lighthouse job, where he worked at night charging the miners' lamps, had disappeared. He had one of the best jobs in the operation; he had very little work to do and had no supervision to speak of. As long as the batteries were charged every morning, the company did not concern itself with questions of whether he might have had a drink while he worked or entertained visitors of the female persuasion.

But when the mine closed and there was no work nearby, Jesse found it hard to justify walking long distances for irregular pay. Like most everyone, he assumed the mine would soon reopen, that the closure was only temporary, but by 1933 it looked like neither Greasy Creek nor the country would be prosperous again, and he began to drink more heavily.

One Sunday morning, Pearl went to church without him, since he had failed to return from a Saturday night bender and rarely went to church with her anyway. She did not stay with her parents for Sunday dinner as she usually did and instead went home when the service concluded. She had decided it was time for a serious discussion with her wayward man. If their marriage were to survive, he would have to straighten up.

As she approached the house, she saw someone, obviously female because she was adjusting her dress, slip out the back door. When she arrived at the front door, she found it locked from the inside. There was a smell of perfume in the air.

"Jesse, open this door," she shouted. There was no answer.

"You son-of-a-bitch," she cursed. "I know you're in there. Open the door."

There was still no response, although she could see the curtains move. She was blindly angry; she had saved what little money she could from whatever Jesse gave her to buy some pretty cloth, something better than feedsack, to make new curtains for the old house. She had cut and sewed and ironed them and made a bedspread to match. That was probably what drove her over the edge: Jesse had soiled their bed forever with whatever rip he had taken in there and she would make him pay.

At the corner of the porch was a claw hammer and, beside it, a bucket of rusty nails; Pearl knew immediately what she would do with it. Picking them up, she began nailing shut all the windows and doors.

"This is your last chance, you whore-hoppin' bastard," she screamed. "I swear, Jesse Hopkins, I'll burn this place down and you in it."

If Jesse thought her rage would abate, he was mistaken; with each nail she drove, it merely intensified. "You hear me, Jesse? I'll burn it down."

She dropped the bucket after the last window had been nailed and began smashing glass with the hammer. With a pack of Diamond matches, she calmly began lighting the curtains she had so lovingly made and pushed them back inside.

"Pearl, are you crazy?" Jesse finally shouted from inside the house. "Help me put out these fires."

"Why?" she shouted back. "You're goin' to burn in hell, any way. You might as well do it now and get it over with."

"Pearl, God damn it, the house is on fire."

Pearl finally became alarmed. She realized, somewhat tardily, that it was not her house to burn and attempted to pull some of the curtains back through the window to stomp them out, but the fire had acquired a taste for the old wood. With only a single bucket on a chain at the well box, there was little chance the flames could be extinguished. The battle, in which Pearl was a reluctant ally to her husband, was lost and the house was consumed.

When Harrison surveyed the damage, he realized that, in a way, this now made it easier for him to divide his property among his children. He offered Rissie her share in Snake Branch hollow, just above the smoking ruins of the home place. Harrison would not rebuild on the site, which was reserved for another daughter, but Rissie was ecstatic with her father's gift. After Mammy's house, the spot Harrison gave her for her own was her favorite place in the world.

In a flat spot beside the creek, there was a giant Buckeye tree that had grown unmolested for at least a hundred years. Although the wood of the tree had some use in making artificial limbs, and Harrison had made peg legs from some of its branches for the boys who lost their own in the mines, it was not oak or poplar. It had escaped the holocaust wrought by the Yellow Poplar Lumber Company and Rissie was thankful: she had spent her childhood in its shade.

With his sons (including Jesse, who owed his father many more debts than just for the incinerated home place) and Harlen's family, the spot soon came to life. Harrison dug a well and lined it with some of the sandstone rocks that had been stacked in huge piles on the hillside since the Old Ones cleared the fields. With more of the rocks, they expanded the flat land beside the creek and built a retaining wall to hold off spring floods. They used more of the rock to build the chimney for Rissie and Harlen's new house.

As the house went up, Harrison plowed up the old top garden for a kitchen garden for Rissie. The young couple would still have use of the fields at the old place, but it would be easier for Rissie to walk up to the garden for a few tomatoes or ears of corn for supper. The garden had not been plowed for seventy years; during the Civil War it was one of many Greasy Creek families had hidden in the woods because of the constant theft of food by hungry soldiers. Surprisingly, once the brush had been cleared away, the earth yielded easily to the plow.

Harrison thought he would lose his bees, but the hives were still working, so he brought them to the hillside above Rissie's new house. He would not have to walk very far to tend them, since he would live with Rissie and Harlen, and honey was too prized to leave his "bee gums" unprotected. At the head of the hollow, the old Sims place was surrounded by a huge orchard, and his bees would benefit by not having as far to go to work the spring blooms.

The barn and hog pen at the old house were far enough from the conflagration that they were not damaged and Harrison gave his cow to Harlen and Rissie, but he built a chicken coop closer so that Rissie could gather eggs when she needed them and wring a chicken's neck when she wanted to have one for dinner.

The new house had four tiny rooms, with hearths in the two front rooms and a kitchen and another room in back. Harlen and Rissie would sleep in one of the front rooms and Marvin in the other. Harrison would sleep in the back room, near the cook stove that she would keep lit all night in winter to keep her father warm.

Although the house was small, Rissie made sure it had a grand front porch, like the porches at her father's and her grandmother's houses, porches where the family could gather on warm summer nights and listen to Harlen play the banjo. It took every dime the young couple had to build their home, but Rissie told Harlen and her father that the next thing she wanted was a fence along the creek. Harlen could make enough money to pay for it if they saved. He would sometimes pack his banjo and head out with his friends on weekends to play dances and honky-tonks for people who still had money. He usually drank up some of what he made, and Rissie would not complain, but now he had to cut back. They would soon need it; although Marvin was old enough not to fall over the rock wall along the creek, it might be dangerous for a younger child. Rissie had an announcement to make: she had a baby on the way.

*   *   *

When Laura Mae received the cable from Union Trust, she considered her options: she could sell out now to the company that actually had voting control of her stock, or she could wait to see what would happen. Although Corrigan-McKinney had a potential suitor in the wings when Laura Mae had her visit with the accountants two years before, things had changed. Ohio industrialist Cyrus Eaton wanted the company and in 1930 had borrowed $23 million to finance the acquisition for his own Republic Steel Corporation. He had put together a sound plan that would create a steel conglomerate that would rival US Steel. He knew the efficiency and profitability of the company Price McKinney had built, and with the last male stockholder in his grave, he thought he could pick it up at a fire sale price.

Everything was in place for him to become a modern Andrew Carnegie, but not all his financing was secured. There was no doubt that he would get it and his Midwest Steel Corporation would pay a handsome price for Corrigan-McKinney, at least that was the prevailing assessment at Union Trust. Laura Mae wasn't so sure. Her proposition to Union Trust was simple: buy me out now and then sell out to Cyrus Eaton when he gets the money. Union Trust, sensing a huge profit, made the deal. It was an unusual deal in the manner of payment, but the company went through with it anyway.

Laura Mae went back to London after placing $21 million in government bonds so she would not have to deal with taxes. She kept another million for spending money; her annual income from the bonds would be about $800,000, but she had to have something to live on now. The $142,500 per year she had been forced to live on since her husband's death was embarrassingly small for someone with her social responsibilities.

As for Union Trust, the profit they anticipated by selling out to Cyrus Eaton never materialized. As the Depression deepened, Eaton found himself unable to secure the last of the financing for his scheme and he was devastated. Adding insult to injury, he was washed out of his own company and replaced by a man named Tom Girdler, whom he had brought into the company.

Although Eaton was no longer at the helm, Girdler recognized the logic in Eaton's plan, but could not implement it until 1935 and Corrigan-McKinney finally became part of Republic Steel, which would go on to become the largest steelmaker in Cleveland.

On Greasy Creek, a few people knew of the drama that was into its final act in Cleveland. Some had heard the company would be sold and were hoping the new owners would resurrect the town. The mine had closed before all the old McKinney Steel signs had been replaced and now a new company would tack up its own signs. In the camp, the paint had peeled from company houses, the streets had filled with mud and the sidewalks had cracked and sunk. The great tram had rusted from lack of use and birds nested in the silent power plant.

The last news most of Greasy Creek had of Corrigan-McKinney was five years before, when Laura Mae sold her share of the company. In Cleveland, twenty guards, armed with pistols and rifles, lined the short route taken by three armored cars that transferred $22 million in cash, from Union Trust to National City Bank. She could have accepted a check, but she could not forgive Union Trust for allowing the price of her stock to drop so far. She had to have greenbacks, she sniffed, because she was not sure in these trying times that checks were all that safe. Besides, how many Clevelanders, regardless of their pretensions or real wealth, had actually seen that much money? They would now, and it was Laura Mae's. If one did not know better, one might assume this was her parting shot at the society matrons who never invited her to tea.

Beside the road are the remains of a concrete pier that supported the base of one of the aerial trams that brought coal down the mountainside to be loaded into gondolas. The mine shut down in 1928 and was never reopened. All the steel was removed in 1940 to melt down into armaments for the coming Second World War.

The Greasy Creek Hotel. Its current owner is salvaging and remodeling the ancient structure into apartments. It is one of two public buildings still standing where once there was an entire town. The other structure is the hospital, now a private home whose residents are completely accustomed to the bumps and rattles of the ghosts of coal miners who died there.

Stardust

"What's wrong with King, Papaw?" I asked my grandfather as I stroked the head of the old dog. I had not seen him poking his nose through the gaps in the fence as he usually did when I made my way up the hollow, but I knew I would find him in the place he loved most, lying in the sunlight on a big flat rock thrust out from the hillside behind the house. This was his favorite spot; the heat eased the pain in his hips. On the occasions I saw him anywhere else, he barely moved, his back legs stilt-like from the arthritis that enfeebled him. On that day, he could not wag his tail, but still managed to raise his nose when I touched him. "Is he sick?"

"No, he's just old, sugar lump," my grandfather replied. "Dogs get old, just like people do."

"How old is he?"

"Well, he's over twice as old as you are. That's right smart old for a dog."

"You reckon he's thirsty?"

"I don't think so."

"You reckon he's hungry?"

"No, he's not hungry."

"He's just old?"

"He's just old."

The next morning, I asked my mother to let me take King some gravy for breakfast, but when I ran around my grandfa-

ther's house, King was not on his rock. My grandmother came out on the back porch when she saw me.

"Where's King?" I asked her. She looked into my eyes before she spoke.

"Ask your papaw," she said softly. I followed her glance to the hillside where I saw my grandfather making his way back down the hill with a mattock in his hand. I ran up the hill toward him, my eyes nearly blinded with tears.

"Where's King, Papaw?" I asked my grandfather, my voice breaking. My grandfather looked at me sadly.

"We found him this mornin'," he said. "He just went to sleep last night and didn't wake up. I took him up there." He turned to point and I rushed past him.

My grandfather followed me to the fresh mound of earth covered by rocks he had just left. I sat down beside the grave and sobbed as he patted me on the back. I didn't want to believe King was buried there. I didn't want to believe he had died. I didn't want to believe anything I loved would ever die.

"Everthing has its time," my grandfather said, kneeling beside me. "Some..." He caught his breath. "Some a little sooner than others," he looked into the distance when he spoke, his own eyes misting. Tears for King, I thought. "But he had him a good life. That's all that matters, and he don't hurt no more."

"He don't hurt no more?" I asked. That made it worse. I hadn't appreciated that he had hurt before.

My grandfather sat beside me until I had no tears left and I stood up. We started walking back and my grandfather's arm was across my shoulders all the way. I sobbed again when I saw the rock he would never sleep on again. I was still holding the bowl of gravy when we got to the bottom of the hill.

*   *   *

Since 1935, when Republic Steel acquired Corrigan-McKinney, labor unions had been legal in the United States, but

Republic's president Tom Girdler refused to have anything to do with them. The Depression was squeezing not only employee paychecks, if not ending them altogether, but corporate profits were declining as well. When Girdler refused to meet with representatives of the fledgling Steel Workers' Organizing Committee in 1937, a strike was called and Republic workers began walking off the job. All across the Midwest, steelworkers were trying to organize a union and when they met resistance, the result was the "Little Steel" strike against the smaller competitors to giant US Steel, which had already signed a contract.

Among the last to leave were the men at the Corrigan-McKinney plant who had been there when Price McKinney built it. They may have retained some loyalty to the company, but when Girdler brought in scab workers and armed thugs, practically all of them walked out. Steel production in Cleveland essentially stopped.

On the advice of Cleveland's Public Safety Director Elliot Ness, Mayor Harold Burton revoked a permit Republic Steel had to land planes containing scab workers near the plant. Soon barricades went up and tensions between workers and scabs rose to the point that the Ohio governor ordered in the National Guard and steel began to roll once more. The Guard was later removed, but violence broke out again in front of the main entrance. It was swiftly quelled and was nothing like the infamous Memorial Day Massacre at Republic Steel's Chicago mill earlier that year, when ten demonstrators were shot in the back by police, but for Clevelanders it left no doubt an era had ended. Some of the men remembered Price McKinney walking through those gates with his baseball team to clobber the boys from Otis Steel, but like an old photograph left too long in the sunlight, that memory and its relevance began to fade.

By the end of August, most of the striking workers had returned. It was inevitable; they had families to feed and had no choice but to take whatever work they could get. Things were never the same at the mill after that; something had been lost on the picket lines, something tangible and real. It was like the death of a friend.

On September 1, Harrison Hopkins died of a stroke. He had been failing since Pearl burned down the home place, but that wasn't the reason for his debility. The last time he had showed any strength was when he was a pallbearer for IB Sanders three years before. IB and Adelaide lived just above Harrison, and were close to him. Although she was younger than Mammy, Adelaide was the best friend of Harrison's mother. And although IB was older than Harrison, IB was in better health. His death from dysentery, a result of the new dangers of so many people living so close together on Greasy Creek, shocked Harrison. Communicable diseases were on the rise since the camp closed; there had been no inoculations on Greasy Creek for years.

Harrison had seen hard times before, times even worse than the Depression, but he had never seen so much resignation. After the good times of the Twenties, so many hopes had been dashed. It seemed to him that the people of Greasy Creek, his people, had nearly given up. The promise of the mines, as he had warned his sons, was not kept. No one was sure if times would ever improve and few people had faith in the future. To Rissie, it seemed like Harrison was not really living in this world anymore, that he was now just passing through, like an uncertain pilgrim, on the way to somewhere else.

The crowd of mourners was too big for Rissie to lay out her father inside the small house he had helped build. Instead, his coffin was placed in front of the big Buckeye tree in her front yard on the same spot she had played as a child and where her children now happily romped. Among the crowd was a black-eyed, thirteen-year-old girl that came with her family for the funeral. She was part of IB Sanders's family and she remembered Marvin coming with his family to IB's funeral.

At the cemetery, Harrison was placed next to Lila's grave, which was marked by a lovely marble stone, professionally cut with the outline of a heart at the top. It was identical to the stone marking Manie Ethel Hopkins's grave. Frank had paid for both of them with his earnings at the Greasy Creek mine, but the mine had been closed for nearly a decade. None of Harrison's children had enough money now to buy him a stone, but as soon as the mine reopened, they said, they would all pitch in and help Frank buy one to properly mark their father's grave. Until then, the traditional method of marking graves was employed: a flat stone from the creek with his name and death date chiseled into it. An untutored hand produced it and the "n" in his last name was reversed. It would be thirty years before Frank would have another stone, better but still homemade, replacing the one gathered from the creek.

As much as she loved her father, Rissie soon realized that for the first time in her life she was truly free. She had taken care of her mother and her father until they died, as everyone expected her to, and she had no regrets about her service, but now she had her own family to raise. Marvin was fifteen when his grandfather died and her daughter Bobbie Jean was four. When their friends and cousins stayed all night with the children, the tiny house had to remain quiet for Harrison's sake. Rissie's demand that Harlen build a fence along the creek proved its worth, as the children took full advantage of the outdoors and played noisily in the yard from daylight until dark. Marvin's dogs, Jack and Farley, the former named for Harlen's father, who had given Marvin the dog, added their barks and yips to the usual pandemonium under the Buckeye. It pleased Rissie that her children loved the spot so much; the only two places in the world she loved more were the porches at her father's house and her grandmother's house and both were gone.

Rissie had noticed something of a change in Marvin since they'd buried her father. After the funeral, Marvin gingerly asked his mother about some of the people who came to pay their respects, especially one family from upper Greasy Creek. He remembered one of the girls in that family from the previous spring.

It surprised him, along with the rest of the Middle Greasy Grade School baseball team, when he saw her warming up with the boys from Upper Greasy Grade School. She looked athletic, but certainly not like a boy. She was tall and almost Indian-like with her rich complexion, black hair and huge black eyes. She had long, coltish legs, runner's legs, and even at thirteen was as tall as Marvin.

So what, he thought? She was still a girl and girls can't play baseball. They must really be in trouble if this is all they can do. He almost made fun of her as the rest of his team did, but something restrained him, especially when he looked into her dark eyes. On her first time at bat, she knocked the ball completely out of the field and into the weeds across the creek, and he had to reevaluate his initial assessment. The Upper Greasy Creek team won handily that day, and he thought he saw her looking at him when they departed for home.

"That's Peter Prater's granddaughter," Rissie said, when Marvin finally got around to asking about her. "Her name is Pansy. Her mother is Aunt Adelaide's niece."

"Boy, she sure can play ball," Marvin said. He already knew her name, but did not know which Prater clan she belonged to. He wondered if her breath quickened as much as his when their eyes caught each other.

School began again after Harrison's funeral, and once again the Upper Greasy Creek Grade School team played Middle Greasy and Lower Greasy schools. Once again, Pansy Prater was the star player for Upper Greasy as they swept the games. The following spring, when the fields dried up enough to play again, Upper Greasy Creek School trounced their competitors yet again. No Middle Greasy Creek boys laughed anymore when Pansy Prater came up to bat; they wished instead she were playing for them. As Marvin watched her dark eyes intensely study the pitcher, he did not know she was searching for his own eyes, blue as an April sky, each time the Upper Greasy Creek Grade School team came onto the Middle Greasy Creek Grade

School field. Some time in the future, she planned to tell him; she did not know that would come sooner than later.

*   *   *

Since the mine closed, changes were occurring on Greasy Creek, in some ways for the better and in some ways for the worse. For the better, the old social conventions were beginning to reestablish themselves: Sunday dinners after church, neighbors coming together to can vegetables or sew quilts, and families gathering on Decoration Day to visit the family cemeteries. For the worse, many family members could no longer attend, since they had gone away in search of work. Sometimes they returned, as disappointed as they were when they left and certainly no richer for the expense of traveling to Ohio or Michigan, but some managed to find jobs and never came back.

In the mines of Pike County, work was irregular and usually only a day or so a week. Men were paid by the tons of coal they loaded, and when they had the chance to load, they worked themselves into exhaustion, coming home only to eat and collapse behind the kitchen stove until they could go back to the job. When a miner took his dinners with him, it was not unusual for him to cease work for a few minutes and eat his simple lunch while evacuating his bowels at the same time. It was an efficient process and it had to be; any time lost from loading coal cost him money.

Harlen took any mining job he could find, but like the rest of the men of Greasy Creek, he rarely made enough money for his family to live on. His banjo brought in some money, when he found a place to play, but he made more delivering whiskey his father made from the still the legendary Elisha Hopkins had used years before. It was a potent brew, but it was not Elisha's. Nobody would ever taste Elisha's whiskey again. The old man had taken his recipe with him to the grave, but Jack Damron's moonshine had its merits, too. It was so highly prized by the miners of Greasy Creek that little of his production was sold elsewhere. Few people could still remember Elisha anyway.

When the Greasy Creek mine closed, Jack expanded his operation and business was good, even after Prohibition was repealed. Harlen had run moonshine for his father and even though he had no regular income, he managed to feed and clothe his family and allow himself an occasional drink. After his father shut down the still, he continued to drink, but only if he had extra money to spend.

One Thursday, Harlen went to the weekly cattle market sale in Pikeville and Rissie, who had saved fifty cents, sent the money with him to buy her a fern. However, the money did not purchase what it was intended for, and on the way home Harlen went through the hills until he found a plant that looked commercial enough to satisfy Rissie.

"Looks kindly puny," she said when he returned with it, but she was happy. She also sniffed his breath knowingly when she took the plant away to repot.

Sometimes Harlen allowed himself more than a drink, and sometimes his striking good looks were just as strong an attraction for the young women of the creek as the whisky he sold to the honky-tonks that dotted Pike County. Harlen had admirers at each location; it was somewhat of an occupational hazard.

On one occasion, news of a particular assignation with one of the ladies of the creek arrived home before Harlen did and he had to retreat to the safety of a far corner of his front porch rather than face the wrath of an infuriated Rissie armed with a poker. He spent the night there with Rissie patiently sitting on the steps, like a cat waiting for a mouse to leave its nest, but by morning she had forgiven him. She always did, since deep inside she knew he loved her more than anything on earth. She still found it hard to believe that the handsomest man on Greasy Creek was her man and no one else's, at least in the final analysis.

But the one fact of which she had absolutely no doubt was that he loved Marvin as if he were his own son. On Marvin's birthday, Rissie demanded that he go to the store to buy something for the boy and some new trousers for himself. She was tired of patching up the holes in his dress pants for funerals. When he returned with his purchases, he proudly displayed his new trousers and gave Rissie some new cloth and a new outfit for Bobbie Jean, who was one year old and unimpressed. Although Marvin said nothing, Harlen could see the corners of his mouth turn down at the slight.

"Harlen, you've teased that baby long enough," Rissie said. "Give him his new clothes."

Beaming, Harlen reached into the bag he had deftly hidden, and produced a new pair of pants, a shirt, and even a new belt. For a moment, Marvin did not know what to reach for, his new clothes or the man who had raised him as a son.

When Marvin grew older, Harlen would sometimes take him along when he went to work in the mines, but would not let him come inside. The summer he turned sixteen, Harlen got him a job picking slate, removing pieces and shards of rock as coal was tumbled through a shaker in a cleaning process. Marvin was paid fifty cents a day and was grinning from ear to ear when the day was done and he came home with his adoptive father, both covered in coal dust, to the house on Snake Branch. Rissie beamed when she saw her men trudge up the road. She had supper on the table waiting for them.

If anyone looked for a reason why Rissie and Harlen were in love, it might not have been clear at first. Certainly, it would not have been her physical beauty, and she would be the first to admit that she was lacking in that regard. Her repaired cleft palate added a whistle to her words and her clubfoot made standing difficult. There were many more attractive girls on Greasy Creek than Rissie Hopkins Damron, and she would admit that too.

But there were none that had the inner glow that entranced Harlen when he first saw her on Malissa Prater's porch. The girls on the creek would be the first to admit that as well. With graceful movements in spite of her infirmity, and the love and pride she had in her children, those girls saw her as the older sister they all wanted to emulate.

But no one would question why Rissie and Harlen loved each other anyway; there were no two people on Greasy Creek so much alike in every other way. They loved to laugh, at themselves as much as anything else, and their house was always full of life and joy.

The young people of Greasy Creek loved their spirit and the old people valued their company. While Rissie could always be counted on to bring food to families during funerals or sickness, she would also share the bounty of her vegetable and flower gardens at any time. She gave hope to all the young women who looked at their own minor infirmities and realized they could be overcome.

The boys of Greasy Creek saw Harlen as their hero, an icon with a chiseled face and near-perfect physique, and he was a natural leader who would never use his strength to force an advantage. The bullies of the creek avoided him, for good reason; too many had found themselves waking up with swollen eyes or missing teeth, remembering only drawing back to deliver a *coup de grace* on some hapless victim and seeing stars before their fists connected with their targets.

My cousin Ival Ratliff, daughter of Frank and Rissie's brother Bud Hopkins told me the kids on Greasy Creek loved to visit Rissie and Harlen because they were "liberal." The teenagers did not use the term then, but they would have known what it meant. And they knew what "sanctuary" meant. The despair of the deserted coal town was forgotten at Rissie and Harlen's house. It soon became the preferred gathering place for Greasy Creek's young people who could yet find hope among the ruins of so many shattered dreams.

In April 1938, both Rissie and Harlen celebrated their birthdays at the same time, as they usually did, but Rissie fried much more chicken than usual. When Marvin returned from a visit to his father, who lived across the mountain, he asked why there was so much food.

"We got some new neighbors, baby boy," she said, somewhat cryptically. "They just moved into the Sims place." The Sims family had bought the two-story, Sears and Roebuck house built by the camp honeydipper who saved his money, but who had moved away the year after the camp closed. Now the Sims family was gone as well and the house had been empty for months. "We're going to take them some supper."

"Who are they?" Marvin asked.

"Oh, you'll see when we get there," Rissie said.

With Bobbie Jean toddling along with them, Harlen, Rissie and Marvin carried bowls of chicken and dumplings, fried chicken, canned green beans from Rissie's pantry, since fresh green beans hadn't come in yet, and cornbread up the hollow. There, in the only other house in Snake Branch, the Andrew Prater family was busy moving into their new home. Marvin was thunderstruck; he would remember that moment for the rest of his life. Snake Branch now became the center of the universe for him. He thought that no place in the world would ever mean as much to him as that tiny hollow.

Earlier that same day in Vienna, half a world away, 200,000 fanatically cheering Austrians welcomed German Chancellor Adolf Hitler into their city to proclaim the Anschluss.

*   *   *

After ten years, the only former Corrigan-McKinney employee still drawing a check on Greasy Creek was nearly forgotten in the vast enterprise of Republic Steel. EB Mullins was officially the caretaker for the camp, but had no budget to maintain it with. In fact, part of his salary was deducted in Cleveland as lease payment for the hotel where EB and his wife lived and kept the post office and a grocery store. EB had a respectable business, especially since the Alka and Greasy Creek post offices had been consolidated, and he wanted to expand. He had an offer for Republic Steel, whose clerks were surprised when they received his request to buy the building.

When the power plant shut down, EB put in coal stoves to keep the place warm and now wanted to install a boiler to put the radiators back into use. He did not want to make the investment in a leased building and he thought he would see if Republic Steel would let it go.

The request may have also surprised Tom Girdler when an assistant brought it to him. With the acquisition of other small steel companies and their coal mines, Republic Steel had also shut down the Wolfpit operation and now both Greasy Creek and Wolfpit were virtual ghost towns, but the ramifications of selling the building far exceeded any authority a clerk would have had. The hotel was central to the town of Greasy Creek, and although the company did not use it for anything, its sale could interfere with the possibility of operating the camp should the mine reopen.

Girdler had already been thinking about the future for Republic Steel and the issue was timely. Although the steel industry was only at 62% of capacity overall, due to flat sales of automobiles, it was still an improvement from last year because of increased military spending. Both domestic and foreign orders had been increasing to shipyards and armaments makers in a duplication of conditions that existed prior to the First World War. If war did break out in Europe, America would be in an excellent position to capitalize on that market.

He was also aware of what had happened the previous year during the Little Steel Strike and had no sympathy for strikers or potential strikers. The problem with a company town is that the labor force would be right at the doorstep of the operation. He would be offering sustenance to the very men who could strike the mines at will. It did not take him long to make a decision.

"All right," Girdler said. "Send some people down to review the situation. If the price seems fair, sell the property to..."

"Mr. Mullins."

"Mr. Mullins. We might as well get something out of that place. Send some engineers along as well. If we do need the coal, I'd like to know how much it would cost to get the mines operational."

"Yes, sir."

"As for reopening the camp," he said. "You may assume that will not happen."

In August of 1938, Republic Steel sold the hotel and some other property on Greasy Creek and Wolfpit to EB Mullins. The sales price of the buildings was a fraction of what they had cost Price McKinney to build, but both Mullins and Republic Steel were satisfied with the deal. The land agent for Republic Steel asked EB to let him know if anyone wanted any of the houses. They would sell the lots with or without the houses and take down what was left. The company had no use for them anymore.

Word that the houses were for sale sped through Greasy Creek and Wolfpit like a rocket. Although the company would not sell any of the office buildings or structures related to the mines, everyone now knew the camp would never reopen. Republic Steel had few takers for the Greasy Creek houses, although Rissie noted one of the houses stood squarely on the spot where Mammy's house once stood and she told Harlen that would be her choice. But she was happy where she was; besides, who would have that kind of money anyhow?

*   *   *

Since Marvin was now sixteen and had his driver's license, EB Mullins hired him to slog the miserable roads out of Greasy Creek to the wholesaler in Pikeville to get groceries for the expanded store. The trains no longer ran and grass grew between the rails and ties. It was a great responsibility for a sixteen-year-old, but EB trusted him. Marvin had a good pedigree; any child of Rissie or Frank would deserve such trust.

John and Bessie now lived in Pikeville, and Marvin made use of the Pikeville trips to check on his aunt and his cousins, especially Bessie's oldest son Caudill, named for John's brother, who was one of the first men killed by the Greasy Creek mine. The younger Caudill looked up to Marvin as his older brother, and Marvin made sure he always had change for a movie or a treat. It was also an opportunity for Marvin to catch a glimpse of Pansy when he could. During the summer, she had often walked by Rissie's house on the way to stay with her Aunt Adelaide and was sometimes lured into the house by Rissie or the kids that gathered there. However, the new school year had begun and Pansy now stayed with Adelaide's niece Effie, Pansy's grandmother, so that she could attend high school in Pikeville.

Both Marvin and Pansy found themselves looking forward to the times she could come home to Greasy Creek, since they now lived so close together, although Pansy's parents were wary of her spending too much time at Rissie's house. They were not quite as trusting as Rissie of teenagers. Still, during the winter away from Greasy Creek, Pansy's fondest memories were of the summer, when lightning bugs floated on the dense summer air, punctuated by the red glow of cigarettes and the soft murmur of voices from Rissie's porch or under the Buckeye. The gatherings at Rissie's house seemed nearly dreamlike to Pansy, and her brother Avery would be among the crowd, usually surrounded by adoring females, since he was very much the masculine version of Pansy's dark good looks.

There was music when Harlen was there to pick his banjo, or even without accompaniment, as the gang would easily break into song. Perhaps they were just happy to have found something bright in the grim world of the Depression, but no one would miss a night at Harlen and Rissie's for anything. Although times were hard, there was always something to eat at Rissie's place: hot popcorn sprinkled with the salty butter Rissie had churned, washed down with Rissie's sweet tea, or doughnuts Rissie would dust with powdered sugar as they drained and cooled on newspapers on the table in the kitchen.

Sometimes in winter there would be a special treat, when Harlen would dispatch the boys to chop up icicles that grew like great stalactites from cliff faces and bring the ice in washtubs to Rissie's porch. Although the temperature might be below freezing, the kids of Greasy Creek would wolf down homemade ice cream as if it were July. Winter or summer, the favorite place for most of Greasy Creek's young men and women was Rissie and Harlen's house, where two generous people often went without things they wanted for the sake of the kids. "Mommy's spent all the money on food again," Bobbie Jean would sometimes complain.

One Saturday, Harlen's brother King Charles Damron brought her a puppy and she had nothing to complain about that night as she carried the hapless animal from guest to guest. The kids all confirmed to her that she deserved it. She was the prettiest little girl on Greasy Creek and she deserved the prettiest puppy.

"What are you goin' to name it, Sissy?" they asked her. She hadn't decided on a name yet, but Marvin suggested "King," since he had named his dog Jack after Harlen's father. After Bobbie Jean went to sleep, the exhausted animal collapsed between Harlen's feet that night.

"Little King," he said, lifting his banjo out of his lap and the puppy into it. "I guess that's your name."

Sometimes in winter, after the food had been consumed and the dishes washed and put away, the kids would sit quietly around the fireplace in the living room and ask Rissie to tell a story. She had many of them, and every girl and boy who sat there would feel a part of the stories, since it was also their families she spoke of, regardless of their names.

On those nights, the ghosts of Greasy Creek were summoned to Rissie's hearth and they came willingly. Old Lige became a real person to the listeners, because they learned he was part of the ancestry they had forgotten they had. Rissie told them of the War, how Lige had tried to keep his brothers out of it, but saw them both march off to different sides and only one return. She told them of brave horsemen riding through the night and sweethearts waiting under moonlit trees for their lovers. She could see the boys' chests swell with pride when she spoke of young men like themselves, believing in a cause even if it caused them to break from their families forever.

She told them of the Indians of Greasy Creek, from whom many in the group were also descended, and how they disappeared when the great trees fell, only to come back one night for a final tribute to the one white man they would have given their lives for. She told them of loyalty and friendship and devotion, and they could almost hear the drumbeats and chanting on Ripley Knob as souls passed into eternity. Her audience allowed themselves to mourn for the lost graves of warriors they never knew.

She could see the girls' eyes misting when she told them of young girls just like them, rereading crumbling old love letters from boys who would never return. She could feel their hearts catch when she told them of Victoria, who married George in spite of the fact that he was a Union soldier and her father died serving the Confederacy. She lived only three days after the wedding and never saw her child grow up, and as the girls would walk home from Rissie's in the cold night air, under stars that seemed so close and so clear they could be picked like blackberries, some swore they could see Victoria's shade gliding off the mountain once more to look for her daughter.

Neither the girls nor the boys knew that during those firelit nights they were being instructed as well as entertained, and they did not know those lessons would be with them for a lifetime. But they began to wonder if there truly was such a place as Rissie said Greasy Creek was so long ago. They had been born in good times they did not know, since they were children then, and had known only hard times since then, and except for a brief interlude of false hope in the town, that was all they ever knew.

Could there have been another time, they began to wonder, a different time? Was there ever a time when men were men, real men, and women were real women and could determine their own fate? Could there have been a time when the trees grew into the sky and eagles lifted easily from their branches to catch the wind? Could there have been an Eden in these hills before the War, before the country was shattered, before the great trees fell, before the coal mines and death and disease invaded their country and their souls? And, save for Rissie and the ghosts on Ripley Knob, could anyone sing a song of Zion if no one remembered it anymore?

Eventually, the winter ended and spring came back to Greasy Creek, and so did Pansy. After school was out in the early summer of 1939, she was again sent by her mother to stay with Aunt Adelaide and Pansy was envious as she watched the crowds gather at the little house on Snake Branch. Pansy was happy with the assignment and often volunteered to check on Aunt Adelaide, even though someone else would be staying the night with her. After one such cursory visit to the old lady, she headed back up Snake Branch and could not believe her ears. She heard what seemed like a full country music band coming from inside Rissie's house.

Earlier that day, Harlen walked up the front steps of the house with an almost-new Crosley Battery Sixty-Two radio. Behind him was Marvin, carrying the batteries themselves. Rissie was stunned.

"Harlen, what have you done?" Rissie asked him.

"Got us a radio, girl," he replied. "These kids want to listen to music."

"Harlen Damron, where did you get the money to buy a radio?" she demanded.

"Well, darlin'," he began. "Work's beginnin' to pick up a little and I'm gettin' tired of goin' out every Saturday night to make a little money. I figured these kids'd like to listen to some real music instead of just me a-plunkin' on my old banjer, so I sold it. Got a good price on this radio, too. It's almost new."

"You sold your banjo?" she asked, not believing he would do such a thing.

"Yep, got a good price for it. Bought some extra batteries, too."

"Harlen..." Rissie did not know what to say.

"Listen, Mother," he interrupted her and spoke seriously. "These are good children. It will be worth it. You mark my words; it'll be worth it."

And it was. The first thing they wanted to hear was the Grand Ole Opry of course, but eventually there was other music in the air. Some of the boys had been to great cities and some had served with the Civilian Conservation Corps and made enough money to buy records to play on hand-cranked Victrolas and not all those records were country music. Sometimes on Saturday nights, after the Opry had gone off the air and there was enough electricity left in the batteries for the group to "radio," they would find other music, music where clarinets and saxophones formed new sounds, new melodies the kids could sway to, and even the fireflies that lit up Rissie's porch seemed to move with the rhythm.

New radio stations were coming on line every day, and many broadcasts came from the ballrooms of great hotels, places the kids could only dream of. Before long, the names of bandleaders became common knowledge, names like Tommy Dorsey, Earl Hines, or Duke Ellington, and the girls absolutely swooned when they heard a band called the Glenn Miller Orchestra.

Harlen would put the radio beside the open window, since the house was so small, and couples would sit on the steps or dance slowly on the porch or walk out into the yard under the Buckeye tree to exchange kisses where no one thought they would be seen. Rissie saw them, of course, and understood. She had the wisdom that Mammy had given her, and now her house was Mammy's place all over again for a different generation, even if it was too small for the gangs that descended on it every Saturday night.

Maybe one of these days, I'll get that empty house where Mammy's house stood, Rissie thought. Look how much room we would have for the children.

But Rissie had no doubt that Mammy's unseen spirit wandered her little house on Snake Branch. She could feel her presence on the porch and under the Buckeye tree and she knew Mammy was happy with the legacy she had imparted to the tiny girl with a cleft palate and a clubfoot and who was never expected to have a family at all.

There will be other families soon, Rissie thought. All these children are growing up. My boy is already a man and he has him a good girl. Times are getting better; we might just pull out of this after all. There might be work again and these boys won't have to go away from Greasy Creek ever again.

In September, as Harlen turned the dial, he stopped on a station that was issuing a news report: German armies crossed the border into Poland. Within a week, Republic Steel sent another crew into Greasy Creek to inspect the mine again. Although coal was needed for the mill in Cleveland that now had more orders than it could handle, the Greasy Creek mine was deemed too expensive to safely reopen. It would be easier to open a new mine from Hopkins Creek, just over the ridge, than to try to shore up the crumbling roof on Greasy Creek.. The company sent out a notice that the entire operation would be scrapped instead: the steel power plant, the overhead tram, the rails inside the mine and even the steam pipes buried underground. Every bit of steel that could be salvaged would be torn out and shipped to Cleveland. Any man who needed work would have it. The company needed coal, but it also needed steel. Scrap steel could be melted far more rapidly than ore could be processed and it had orders that needed to be filled now.

To the people of Greasy Creek, this was their final abandonment. To Republic Steel, Greasy Creek was now nothing more than a good source for scrap metal: Price McKinney had put enough steel into the operation to equip an armored battalion.

*   *   *

She had watched him walk away that day, early in the morning, and shoo King back to the house. "Rissie, call the dog," he demanded. "He can't go with me." Harlen was heading off to work as if there really was work again in the mine, as if coal would be dug and picked and loaded and shipped north. But there was no coal coming out of the mine; instead, lengths of rails appeared, rusted from years of disuse, but barely worn by the brief time they were in service. Not one piece of track had been in the mine long enough to replace, Harlen told her. It was such a shame, he said, to have to take them up.

Ain't it dangerous, she had asked him, with that old top? Couldn't if fall anytime? You could get killed there, she told him.

No, baby, Harlen had said, we'll be in and out before you know it. If I do get killed, you got insurance, but I ain't going to die there.

And he didn't, but he died in the hospital from pneumonia that set in after he was injured. His shift was over and he was walking out when the rock fell, fracturing his occipital plate and knocking out two teeth, perfect teeth with neither a filling nor a cavity. It had been two days since he was struck and the fever had set in. The doctors said his time was near.

"We got to talk, Mother," Harlen managed to say, although his dry lips and tongue made it difficult for him to speak. Rissie wiped his face with a cool washcloth, and squeezed drops onto his tongue.

It broke his 'swallow,' Rissie told me. She pronounced it "swaller"; he couldn't 'swaller' nothin'.

"They said I ain't got much time," Harlen said. "So you listen to me. You take the money and buy the house...buy the house where your Mammy lived. You always wanted it. They'll tear down all the rest of those old houses, but you keep the one you want. You make a deed so it'll fall to you or Bobbie if the other one marries first."

"Harlen, I don't..."

"You need a good house, Mother, better than that little place in Snake Branch, and if you don't get it somebody else'll get it and..."

His mind began to drift; the infection had reached his brain.

"...and you'll never be happy up there. You give it to Marvin or sell it to Frank. He don't need to be rentin' no more. He's got a wife and baby, too. It'll be a good place for them. You'll have enough room to take care of your daddy, too."

In his delirium, he had forgotten that Harrison was already gone.

"Now Marvin's grown," he continued. "He'll be fine. You raised him right."

"You raised him too, Daddy. He's yours too."

"He'll only have one daddy again..."

"You'll always be his daddy, too..."

Rissie stood beside the bed, dipping the washcloth into a pan of cool water and wiping his face as he slipped away. Marvin stood beside her, holding her as a son should as his mother speaks to his father for the last time. Frank stood behind Marvin, holding on to the only son he had left in the world, the son who was also saying goodbye, goodbye to his father, his other father. He was a man now and they had all taught him to act like one. All of them had: his mother, his fathers; the mother he never knew.

At the foot and on the other side of the bed with Harlen's brothers, all of whom could not will away the fact that their

198

brother was dying, could not wake up from the dream, the nightmare that everyone in the room was having. The hallway was filled with Harlen's friends and family. *So soon, too soon, they all thought. He just turned thirty-four.* The hospital had never seen so many people waiting at one time, but they were all peaceful, respectful. They were all from Greasy Creek.

"He tried to swaller'," Rissie said. "And all that blood and corruption came up all over his chest. I wiped it away and cleaned him up."

She was a good wife to the end. Not until he was presentable did she allow herself to break down. Not until he was presentable did she allow anyone to see her husband.

It was April and between their birthdays when he died. She would never celebrate her birthday again. She was thirty-six. Harlen Damron was the last man killed by the Greasy Creek mine. *It was April when he died, she told me. It was April when he died. It was April.*

She buried him on the Old Prater above her father, above the all the Hopkinses and the Praters and Mr. Bracken. She saved a place at his feet for herself when her time came. She bought him a marble stone as white as her mother's and Manie Ethel's and she kept it cleaned as long as she could climb the hill to the cemetery. Her son kept it clean thereafter. On starlit nights, it stood out from all the others. It seemed to glow.

A year after Harlen died, bowing to the inevitable, Tom Girdler finally signed Republic Steel to a contract with the union. At the same time, in negotiations that were far less contentious, Republic Steel sold Rissie the camp house she always wanted. The company tore down all the remaining houses on her lot. Her house sat squarely where Mammy's house sat before the camp came to Greasy Creek, before Price McKinney started his model town there, before the living thing that was the town turned to dust and disappeared in the wind.

By December, another wind began somewhere in the Pacific and rolled across the country. No one on Greasy Creek had ever heard of Pearl Harbor, but they would never forget it. Neither would they forget the lost town, not as long as Rissie could speak of it and people would listen.

She offered to give the Snake Branch house to Marvin, but he had registered for the draft by then. If anything happened, he told her, he did not want the property to be tied up with a dead soldier. He did not want to leave Pansy with such a responsibility. He was that much like his fathers, and the one still living wondered why his son would have to fight the same war he did a generation before. *But no one can control anything anymore, Frank thought. Maybe they did once, maybe Rissie could see far enough into the past that she could speak of it, but not anymore; that world is gone forever.*

For some reason, King would not go with them when they moved to the camp; he kept running back to the house on Snake Branch. Frank, who had moved his wife and Marvin's other sister into it, told Rissie to let him stay. He would take care of the dog.

Rissie let him go.

Dogs are that much like people, she thought. That was where his heart was, that was where he would wait for his master as long as he lived. Everything has to have its hope, she thought. Everyone has to have a dream, no matter how impossible. Everyone has to have a heaven to wait for.

Epilogue: Ripley Knob

I *still cannot see them, but I know they are there, up on the mountain or on the lost streets of the town. Below the peak on Ripley Knob, they are at the face of the mine, donning their brand-new hard hats and lamps and climbing into the mantrip, ready to go into the darkness to work in constant danger for the sake of their families. They are telling the old jokes again, recounting the old stories of great deeds and men. They are not unhappy as they wait.*

They are also running the great tram, where the crumbled black blood of the mountain is carried out in huge buckets and loaded onto McKinney Steel coal gons for shipment to Cleveland for its immolation. Or they may be with Jesse at the lamphouse, getting stoned on the fumes and entertaining a lady of questionable virtue. Of course, the mantrip is gone and the tram is gone and only broken glass remains where the lamphouse would redirect the sunlight into the town, but they are there nonetheless.

They may be further up Ripley, firing up Elisha's still, or waiting anxiously on the point, watching for riders to approach, hands nervously fingering triggers, and speaking of the coming war. They may be sitting in the door of his cabin listening to the hounds, even though there is no trace of the still or the cabin or the hounds. There is almost nothing left on Greasy Creek to confirm what happened before the mine came and there is little left to confirm what happened later. In the valley below old Ripley, seven houses remain from over a hundred that my great-grandfather Peter Prater built for Price McKinney. Beyond that, a concrete slab or two, pieces of a foundation, a lonely chimney base give faint testament to the past. Of all the company buildings, only the hospital and the hotel still stand, but no longer a hospital or a hotel. Their current residents are comfortable with the ghosts that visit occasionally.

There is practically nothing left, and there is everything. Every house, every story, every soul my grandmother told me of is still there; I just cannot see them in the corporeal forms that no longer exist. But they did exist. They lived and breathed and died, and somewhere on Greasy Creek they are still there, still living, still loving, still waiting for their young men to come home from the mine or from war.

After his war, my father returned to my mother. He was lucky; he survived. Too many of the Boys of Greasy Creek did not come back from that one. Marvin restarted his life and built his home on the spot where my great-grandfather Harrison Hopkins raised his family, where my grandfather came back to after surviving his own Europe in flames.

My father took a job mining Price McKinney's coal for Republic Steel not far away, where another camp was built with salvaged lumber from Greasy Creek, but it was nothing like Greasy Creek. It was not a town. It was built mostly for the supervisors in the mine; Tom Girdler and the rest of the steel captains had decided that miners could find their own way to work if they wanted a job. No coal camps were built after the Depression, but no one would ever build a camp like Price McKinney's anyway. There was no place for social progressives in big business anymore, no place for Junior Mechanics Lodges sponsored by the company or free typhoid inoculations for everyone in the camp.

There was stillness when the mine closed, but the old men would tell me they could still hear the ursine bellow of the town *if they tried. Perhaps that was true; perhaps they actually could discern something beyond a signature chemical in the brain. Maybe they could still pick up faint echoes as they bounced back and forth across the canyon. Maybe those echoes will be there forever, growing fainter with each rejection, but never fully gone. I can neither see nor hear such things, but if I could, I believe I would hear Price McKinney cheering on the Greasy Creek baseball team or the Greasy Creek brass band warming up for its Fourth of July concert. I might also be able to hear Harlen Damron's banjo above the crowd.*

Girdler's ghost would certainly not be there and neither would Laura Mae's, but I think Jimmy Corrigan's would be, standing near his old trustee, his father's best friend, listening to him chat with Peter Prater and IB Sanders about the future of Greasy Creek, along with all the men who gave him a good day's work for a good day's pay. Price McKinney may have forgiven him by now.

My grandmother Rissie eventually married again, to a widower who was a grandson of Granny Malissy. He had young children to raise and she raised them in the house on the spot where Mammy helped raise most of Greasy Creek three generations before. There are no pictures of Mammy, but I need only a picture of Rissie to see what she looked like, at least at heart. She would have shared the same glow as Rissie, the same aura that smote Harlen, and still today that is all that people remember about my grandmother. Her infirmities are absent in these recollections.

Mammy's house was torn down for the camp after she died on New Year's Eve 1912, and the house that was built there, Rissie's house, was torn down after she died in 1977. We buried her according to her wishes on the hill above that house, supposedly because she and her second husband would be buried together when he passed, but that was not the real reason and he was buried elsewhere anyway. What Rissie wanted was for her family to keep the property forever, but it was sold soon after she died. When the Old Prater Cemetery was moved for road construction, I took her up from her lonely grave and placed her beside Harlen in the new cemetery. Rissie did not know that the Old Prater, the cemetery she told William Bracken would never change, would disappear one week in 2003. But she had been away from Harlen for 63 years. It was time.

If I permit myself, or deceive myself enough, I can almost catch a glimpse of her camp house in the corner of my eye. It is not there, of course, but houses can be ghosts too, and I will sometimes see its spectral walls as I drive by on the way to somewhere, anywhere else. It was a comfortable place, and so was the tiny house on Snake Branch.

In 1973, my grandfather Frank died in that house and we buried him on the Old Prater next to the young woman he had loved and lost fifty years before. Thirty years later, all of the Hopkinses and Praters buried there were taken up from the cemetery and moved away. The house on Snake Branch is gone too, along with the great Buckeye tree that stood in front of it. The whole hollow I grew up in is covered with two hundred feet of rock and fill for the new road, the same road that obliterated the Old Prater. People who glide above it in automobiles will not suspect anything important could have happened there.

When they exhumed the Hopkinses and the Praters, I sent William Bracken's dust back to Muhlenberg County where his wife was buried in 1898. Because I still had family graves to pull from the earth, I could not go with him. To compensate for his lonely journey and my failure to keep the promise I made to Rissie to watch over his grave, I arranged a memorial service in 2005 and met his family. It was the first time any of them had seen his tombstone. It was the first time many of them had seen each other; no Brackens live in Muhlenberg anymore. It was the first time I had met any of them, and none of us had been to Sarah's grave. None of us knew the old man's wife had somehow kept inviolate the place beside her for over a century, as if she knew her man would somehow return. He had been away from her for 105 years. It was time.

Bracken's daughter Mary Jane died in 1946, the year I was born, and she was buried across the state from her husband and her two sons. If their spirits are together, I suspect they are in Muhlenberg instead of Floyd County, where her men died so awfully. But they could be on Greasy Creek too. Granny Malissy told Rissie that ghosts come back to where they were happy, like Lige, who was happiest on Ripley Knob. I know that for a short time, Mary Jane and her family were happy on Greasy Creek. At one time all the families of Greasy Creek were happy there. Although it makes no sense to say so, I suspect Ripley Knob was happy as well.

Granny Malissy died the same year my grandfather buried King. I knew nothing of what my great-great-grandmother would mean to me then; I did not know the epic life she had lived. Neither did I know who had loved the old dog before I did. I might have been told, but I did not take the stories to heart. I was seven years old when they died; I had no pipe on which to tap out their stories. I was not Rissie; I wept only for King.

In Cleveland, the great mills that burned coal from the hills of Kentucky have nearly disappeared, except for the plant Price McKinney built when the last century was young and the future was awash in promise. There seemed to be something about it that gave its different owners hope. Although changed many times, expanded and modernized as the decades passed, it is still there; it is still Price McKinney's, even if few Clevelanders alive can remember the titan who built it or can speak of his deeds. Perhaps he wanted me to tell his story after all.

All these tales of steel, of coal, and of men and women, took place while Ripley Knob watched over Greasy Creek. The peak itself cannot be seen from the valley floor, but it saw everything that happened below it and saw the moon rise above it for 200 million years. It was standing when the Hebrews went into *captivity and was standing when they were delivered from bondage. It was standing when the Indians made their first campfires on its ridge; it was standing when the white men claimed it for their own. It did not flinch when the great poplars were sheared from it, when the first wound was made into its side or when the first soul was released from deep within its womb. It watched over the crippled little girl who came there to tend the graves of people she never knew, but whose stories were important to her. If a mountain can remember, it will not forget her as long as it stands. It will not forget anything.*

Ripley Knob still watches over Greasy Creek, but I do not know for how long. Mountains are as impermanent as people in the coalfields anymore. If the mining operation that has taken most of Price McKinney's Hopkins Creek coal comes closer, grinding and blasting and devouring the ridge as so many other mountains have been shattered and pushed into oblivion, it may too disappear. But like the town I cannot see or the ghosts who will not reveal themselves to me, it will still be there, because once it was there, because once it did exist. That fact may be neglected, it may be ignored or forgotten, but it cannot be denied.

All things have a heart, Rissie would tell me, just like everyone has a soul and everyone has a Jerusalem toward which that soul is tending. Deeds cannot be erased just because they are forgotten. Somewhere, there is a place where such stories are kept, where vigils are maintained, where ghosts will gather.

Even a mountain will have a heart, she would tell me.

Even a mountain will have its Zion.

Printed in the United States
136469LV00003B/6/P